BONDS OF
WIRE

Pencil sketch of the author by
Lieutenant John Lundquist, USAAF.
Drawn while a prisoner-of-war in
Stalag Luft 3, Sagan, Silesia, January 1945.

BONDS OF
WIRE

A MEMOIR

KINGSLEY BROWN

COLLINS
TORONTO

First published in Canada in 1989
by Collins Publishers
100 Lesmill Road
Toronto, Canada
M3B 2T5

Copyright © 1989 by Kingsley Brown

CANADIAN CATALOGUING IN PUBLICATION DATA

Brown, Kingsley, 1911-
  Bonds of wire

1st ed.
ISBN 0-00-215972-4

1. Brown, Kingsley, 1911-   . 2. Stalag Luft 3
(Concentration camp), Zagán, Poland.   3. World War,
1939-1945 – Prisoners and prisons, German.
4. World War, 1939-1945 – Personal narratives,
Canadian. 5. Prisoners of war – Poland – Biography.
6. Prisoners of war – Canada – Biography. I. Title.

D805.G3B76 1989   940.54'72'430924   C89-093005-8

Illustrations: Katherine Taylor
Design: Scott Richardson
Printed and bound in Canada

*To my wife Marion, from the
prisoner in her heart*

Marion and Kingsley Brown,
RCAF Station Trenton,
March 1940

Contents

Acknowledgements

The author is indebted to the late Irene Irwin Clarke, his English teacher at Malvern Collegiate Institute in Toronto, who pushed him into the world of journalism, and as well to Jane Dewar, who when editor of Legion Magazine persuaded him that his prisoner-of-war years were worth writing about.

Foreword

For years, journalist Kingsley Brown has been tempting us with enough snippets of his prisoner-of-war experiences to make us want to yell at him to get cracking and give us the full story.

This he has finally done; it has been worth the wait.

What makes this book doubly bountiful is that accounts by Canadians of prisoner-of-war life in World War II are lamentably few: magazines have carried some of Len Birchall's horror stories of the Japanese camps, and an anthology of reminiscences by members of the Canadian National Prisoners of War Association was published in Victoria in 1985. Now we have a fully-drawn solo portrait — and far different from what you might expect.

Brown was shot down over Europe in 1942 and spent nearly three years in the bag, mainly in Stalag Luft 3, the German POW camp for air force officers. His jaunty message for those of us who, luckily, made it back to England after every raid —

more or less intact — is: you missed the best part of the war.

Granted, Stalag Luft 3 was probably the least bad of all the German camps. Even so, Brown seems to have had, if not fun, enough diverting and entertaining experiences, such as a part-way drive to prison in a Mercedes-Benz, and a brief escape, to make camp life bearable, sometimes even enjoyable. He found his captors, by and large, reasonable, including a Gestapo officer. He has retained his happy memories and discarded (or suppressed) the sad ones, perhaps because, as he says, a prisoner won respect and good repute from his fellows by only one measurement. That was his contribution to the morale and well-being of the prison community, whether by telling a good joke or digging an escape tunnel.

During the "death march," near war's end, when the Germans were trying to keep their prisoners from being liberated by the Russians (to use as hostages?), Brown and his friends managed a sleigh ride, and heard German school children sing to them — in English. (It was the Russians who freed them in a delirious moment of laughter and tears.)

Brown surmounted prison life and he tells us, clearly and freshly, how it was done. Despite his thesis that being a prisoner-of-war is character-building, I'm still glad I wasn't shot down.

Dave McIntosh
Ottawa

Preface

This book has no political statement to make. I have never been able to arrive at any clear judgement as to the good or evil of what I experienced during my German years, apart from the all-embracing evil of war itself. I have no way of knowing how many others may have found a Gestapo interrogation ending on a note of friendly banter, or who may have struck a brief and tenuous comradeship with soldiers of an SS division. These are memories that for me refuse to go away.

Nor can I forget a young refugee German mother, bombed out of her home by Allied airmen, who called me a "terrorist" and a "baby killer," yet showed me a kindness and warmed me with a smile.

The years at Stalag Luft 3 were years for learning about people, years for sharing the deep warmth of comradeship in adversity, years in which so many of us made the discovery that war, and all the vicious propaganda that goes with it, could not extinguish that imperishable bond that links us all, friend and foe alike.

The narrative in this book may help to explain what I mean.

Antigonish,
Nova Scotia
1988

I

Officers Travel First Class

On the morning of July 3, 1942, I awoke in a strange bed with all the symptoms of a hangover. This was not an uncommon experience for air force officers operating from Great Britain in 1942. We were frequently waking in strange beds and more often than not had hideous hangovers. The war would have been unbearably monotonous had it been otherwise. I was neither distressed nor alarmed.

It was not until my glance had wandered up-

ward from the starched edge of an immaculate
pillowslip to the white plaster wall opposite, and I
found myself staring at an almost life-size photograph of *Reichsmarschall* Hermann Göring, that I
recalled with a start just what had gone on the
night before.

It had been quite a party.

It had all started about an hour after midnight
when the bomber I was piloting had been shot to
pieces by the cannon of a Messerschmitt 110 night
fighter. The only survivor, I had come to earth in
my parachute, and the Germans had corralled me
within minutes of my landfall. I had dropped into
the little Dutch town of Staveren, on the shore of
the Ijsselmeer.

There had been a few unnerving moments
when I had been surrounded by a squad of armed
men, seeming all the more sinister in the dark of
the still summer night. They came on motorcycles.
The lights of the cycles, which were reflected on the
barrels of a half-dozen machine-pistols pointed in
my direction, made an eerie vault of the trees over-
hanging the road. The motorcycle engines stopped,
and there was what seemed like an eternity of
silence.

Then one of the squad went through a pantomime to warn me of what might happen if I tried
to run away. He lifted one foot after another,
simulating a running man, and then raised his gun.

"Bang, bang, bang!" he said.

He did look and sound a little comical, and one
of his comrades began to laugh. The pantomimist
lowered the gun, looked around at the others and

then began to laugh too. I suddenly felt a whole lot better and joined in the laughter.

One of the soldiers came close to me and put a tentative hand on my shoulder. He said something that was obviously a question, but I couldn't understand his German. One of the others came to his aid.

"Er . . . you hurt . . . voondit?"

I shook my head. I did have a few scratches. Some flying fragment of metal had made a slight superficial cut in the back of my neck, and I could feel something like scraped skin on my left arm, but I didn't feel like making a fuss over it.

One of the soldiers motioned me over to a motorcycle equipped with a sidecar. The man who had essayed a few words in English flashed his light on the manufacturer's insignia on the fuel tank of the bike. I recognized it at once.

"Goot bike," he said with a wide grin. The others gathered around him, as if to savour my reaction. "*Ja* . . . goot bike . . . BSA . . . see?" He ran a finger under the BSA logo. "Mate in Englant . . . goot bike . . . we get in Dunkirk."

He looked at me and laughed.

I looked back at him and patted the machine approvingly. "Good bike," I said, and the men nodded their heads in unison.

They helped me into the sidecar of the bike, and our little motorcade proceeded down the road and into a more built-up area, halting before some kind of public building. My companions signalled me to get out of the sidecar, and we climbed a few steps to the door of the building.

The bright light inside dazzled me for a moment. We entered an office, warm with old panelling and gracefully aging furniture. There were two or three men in civilian dress, one of whom advanced to shake my hand. Several of the German soldiers had joined the group, and everybody seemed to be talking at once. I found it most confusing. Finally, the soldier who had spoken a few words of English pointed at the civilian who had shaken my hand.

"*Bürgermeister,*" he said.

No one had much English, but they succeeded in explaining that I was in the little Dutch town of Staveren, on the Ijsselmeer, and that this was the town hall.

I was still in a state of confusion. Only an hour earlier I had been in the cockpit of an aircraft fifteen thousand feet overhead. Now I was in a brightly lighted Dutch town hall with a clattering cluster of Germans and Dutch. The man who had been introduced as the *Bürgermeister* led me to a desk where a large guest book lay. He picked up a pen and handed it to me. I was too dazed to determine what it was all about, but since everybody was smiling or laughing and getting on so well together I couldn't see any harm in signing my name in the guest book.

When I put down the pen, the *Bürgermeister* shook my hand again, smiled happily and began talking to me in his native tongue. The room was full of good humour and a lot of tobacco smoke; it reminded me of a Rotary Club luncheon back home. I made up my mind that I was not going to be shot after all.

Seated again in the sidecar of the motorcycle, I was taken for a short ride through the dark streets of the town, to what appeared to be the barracks of the local German garrison. I had the impression that it flanked the waterfront. It was a cosy sort of place. About a dozen men of varying rank were sitting around an orderly room. It was a much more comfortable spot than I suspected a proper Wehrmacht orderly room had any right to be.

"Beer?"

Somebody handed me a bottle of beer and waved me into a chair. Several of the others were also enjoying a beer. There was some cheese on a table, and bread, and a small wooden tub half-filled with pickled eels.

Expectant and curious faces were turned in my direction.

"You married . . . got wife?"

"*Ja . . . ja,*" I said.

"Photo? You got photo?"

I had a snapshot of my wife and four children in a small leather wallet in the pocket of my battle-dress tunic. I took it out and handed it to my interlocutor. The picture was passed from hand to hand around the room and back to me. I returned it to my wallet.

That was the signal for all the others in turn to produce photos of wives and children. As I studied each one I made admiring noises in my throat and nodded approvingly. One of the group produced no photo. He sat quietly in his chair and showed little interest in what was going on. After a pause in the chatter, one of the men looked at me and nodded in his direction. A sudden unease settled over everyone.

"No *Kinder* . . . *verstehen?*"

I didn't understand. I saw that most of the others were looking at the floor, or at their finger-nails. I was conscious of the fact that they weren't looking at me. And the fellow with "no *Kinder*" sat impassive and still, staring straight ahead.

One of the others spoke.

"*Kinder tot* . . . *kaput* . . . dead."

I had a premonition of what was coming.

"*Britische* bomber . . . Köln . . . *Kinder kaput.*"

I wished I hadn't heard. I looked at the man and saw that he was now looking at me. I was embar-rassed. I saw no sign of hatred; there was nothing there. The man just stared at me, with no expres-sion at all. I shook my head and said, "I'm sorry," although I knew my apology was meaningless. I felt miserable. A scraping of chair legs ended the pain-ful silence, and one of the men went over to the table, picked up a pickled eel and held it in front of me.

"*Gut essen,*" he said. "*Gut essen.*"

I was grateful for his intervention. I had never eaten eels of any kind, but I was now so anxious to break the spell of unease that I would gladly have eaten anything to do so. I bit into the eel and made a pleased face, and bit again. I sensed that all the others were as relieved as I was to be shed of the embarrassment. There was more bread and cheese and several more beers, and some humorous at-tempts at conversation, until finally my hosts showed me the neat little iron cot in an alcove off the orderly room and left me to rest.

In the morning, after I had recovered from the shock of looking *Reichsmarschall* Göring in the face, I was handed a razor and permitted to shave in an adjoining washroom. There was a breakfast of good crisp bread with creamy Dutch butter, and coffee. A little later a medium-sized bus, coloured Luftwaffe blue, arrived in front of the orderly room door.

"Good morning!"

The Luftwaffe officer in charge of the party in the bus spoke excellent if accented English. And it was a good morning. The sun was well up, and the day promised to be warm and pleasant.

"We go to Leeuwarden," I was told. I knew about Leeuwarden. It was the Luftwaffe's foremost fighter base, home of the deadly Messerschmitt 110s, which nightly preyed on marauding British bombers. We had a drive of about eighty kilometres ahead of us. About a half-dozen Luftwaffe officers were riding in the bus, and I had the immediate impression that they were along merely for the ride. It would make a nice excursion on a pleasant summer day. They seemed to be savouring the prospect and smiled at me cheerfully as I boarded the bus.

For a few kilometres the highway threaded through green acres of flat farmland, then debouched upon the open coast of the Ijsselmeer, which it followed until it reached the eastern terminus of the famous Afsluit Dijk, the great dike separating the Ijsselmeer from the North Sea.

The officer who was acting as my escort said something to the driver, and the bus turned off the main highway and rumbled along an approach to the dike works. The bus stopped on a little height from which there was an unobstructed view of the project.

"Come. We get out here."

We left the bus and gathered in a little group to look at the dike. I was transfixed. It was like nothing I had ever seen before. In an imperative straight line the dike stretched out into the sea and vanished beyond the horizon. It was as if it had no end.

The Luftwaffe officer explained it to me.

"See, on this side, here, is the Ijsselmeer. Is fresh water, mostly. On the other side is the Nordsee . . . er, you say North Sea. Yes?"

On the Ijsselmeer side a light breeze raised little more than ripples, sparkling in the sunlight, but in the North Sea the darker water was splashed with white caps. Despite the war, work was still progressing on the great dike, and at intervals one could see all the way to the horizon cranes and derricks. We could also see trucks and machinery moving about.

"In future," said the Luftwaffe man, "some day, they will . . . er . . . what's the word? *ja*, pump . . . will pump water from Ijsselmeer . . . make all new land, no more Ijsselmeer . . . new land . . . war against the sea, *ja? Ach*, it is . . . it's *wunderbar!*"

That word I knew. I agreed with him.

"*Ja, wunderbar*," I said. I had never felt quite so cosmopolitan.

The others in the party were chatting and pointing, shaking their heads in unbelieving admiration and muttering "*wunderbar*" over and over again. Every once in a while one of them would turn to see how I was taking it all. They seemed to be enjoying every minute of the occasion, and I had an unmistakeable feeling that they wanted me to enjoy it with them.

I was almost on the point of laughing. I was the prisoner of these men, an enemy; yet they were making it so easy for me to forget that fact. My imagination got the best of me. Suddenly I became a VIP and this was my military guard of honour. I was a foreign dignitary on a state visit, on a formal tour of inspection. The Luftwaffe officer continued to brief me with all kinds of astounding engineering details about the dike and, as befitted my new imaginary status, I listened with an air of grateful gravity.

We spent all of a half-hour admiring the Afsluit Dijk. Then we all climbed back into the bus and started once more on the road to Leeuwarden. We were humming smoothly along the highway when there was a loud, crashing noise and the bus braked to a sudden stop.

"*Achtung!* Second front!"

Several of the Germans put on a show of mock panic for my benefit. The prospect of any Allied "second front" in Europe was a standing joke in Germany. While the driver went back along the highway to retrieve the metal ladder that had come loose from the rear of the bus, some of the officers asked me if I really believed there ever would be a second front.

I could only laugh, and when all the laughter had subsided somebody offered me a cigarette and lit it for me.

It was about noon when we reached the big base at Leeuwarden. As the bus swung through the gates I had a glimpse of Messerschmitt 110s drawn up on the tarmac and couldn't help wondering which one had met me in the skies over the Ijsselmeer the previous night. We dismounted from the bus in front of the officers' mess, where I was given lunch.

Before we sat down, another Luftwaffe officer, who had not been with us on the bus, approached me with a considerable show of embarrassment and told me that I should have to surrender my flying clothes. He took away my sheepskin Irvine jacket — it was minus one entire sleeve, which had been torn off when I left the aircraft — and my long leather gauntlets.

"It's the campaign in Russia," he said. "We need all the warm clothes we can get. I'm sorry."

He glanced for a moment at my flying boots. They were superlative boots, of kangaroo hide, which I had bought from an Australian airman for ten dollars. I should have loathed to lose them. He looked at them for a moment; then shrugged his shoulders and told me I might keep them. He apologized for taking my flight jacket.

I was served a good steak, with a mountain of mashed potatoes and a lot of gravy, and the officer who had been my escort on the bus ride informed me that after lunch I should be sent by train to Amsterdam.

"Perhaps a few days in Amsterdam," he said. "Then you will go to a permanent camp — a Luftwaffe camp, in Deutschland."

As we were leaving the mess hall, one of the Luftwaffe officers stopped me at the door. It appeared he had something to tell me. His English was perfect.

"Before you go, I thought that perhaps you might like to know who shot you down."

I told him I would.

"You were shot down by no less than a prince," he said, smiling in a rather amused way. "Yes, a real prince. He is also one of our top-ranked night fighter pilots — in fact, second only to Major Lent. The man who shot you down is Prince Egmont zu Lippe-Weissenfeld, rank of *Hauptmann.* Would you like me to write that down for you?"

He drew a small looseleaf notebook from his pocket and with very neat strokes of his fountain pen made the notation. He tore out the page and handed it to me.

"Yes, it was a real prince who shot you down. From a family older than the Hohenzollerns." He laughed again in his amused way. "It's a pity you won't have an opportunity to meet him. He is still sleeping. He was pretty busy last night, as you know. Ah, well, when this trouble is over perhaps you can visit us again, in better times."

I thanked him. I never did get to meet the prince who shot me down. Lippe-Weissenfeld met his *Heldentod* — the "hero's death" — about a year later in the troubled German skies.

We emerged from the front door of the mess into the bright afternoon sunshine. There was an open Mercedes staff car waiting at the curb, with a driver at the wheel and a young soldier armed with a tommy-gun holding one of the rear doors open. I guessed he was to be my escort on the journey to Amsterdam.

It was a pleasant drive, aside from the fact that I had no cap and my hair was blowing wildly in the wind. The day was warm and the sky without a cloud. I felt fine. The meal in the officers' mess had been good, and I was enjoying the ride. For the first time in my life I was riding in the famous Mercedes, a car of which I had heard so much. And it was an open Mercedes, and I was actually driving through the Dutch countryside in it, with a chauffeur at the wheel. Several times I thought about the events of the night before and decided that it was good to be alive, riding in a Mercedes in the sunshine.

At the Leeuwarden railroad station my guard showed his transport papers to the attendant at the gate, and we moved onto the platform where the train to Amsterdam was waiting. Compartment doors were swinging open and shut as passengers boarded. A few yards down the platform, the guard nudged my elbow and with a jerk of his head indicated that I was to board the train. The door of the compartment was marked with a big 3. We were travelling third class.

I was barely inside when a sharp shout made me turn around. The young guard was still on the platform but no longer facing me. He was standing at attention before another uniformed figure, who by the tone of voice was quite clearly giving him a reprimand. I was then still ignorant of German rank badges, but there was no mistaking that this newcomer was an officer.

The guard suddenly turned, grabbed me by the

sleeve and hauled me back outside. Now a party of three, we marched along the platform, coming to a halt in front of a door emblazoned with a shining gold 1. With something of a begrudging please-yourself shrug, the guard waved me inside, and he and the officer followed.

We had the compartment to ourselves. It had all the plush elegance of a typical European first-class carriage. I sat comfortably on one side while the guard and the officer sat side by side facing me. The guard was quite impassive, settling back as if he were happy to resign his responsibility to his superior.

The officer studied me for a moment or two.

"My English," he said, "is . . . ah, not good. I have not much practice."

He pointed to the "Canada" flash on the shoulder of my battledress tunic.

"You are Canadian, *ja?*"

"Yes, Canadian," I said.

"And a captain?" My flight lieutenant's stripes were also visible.

"Flight lieutenant," I said.

"*Ja.* In Germany, we say *Hauptmann* . . . is same as captain . . . me, too, am *Hauptmann* . . . a captain."

"Yes," I said, and repeated the word after him — "*Hauptmann.*"

There was a silence, and I had the impression that my *Hauptmann* was trying to marshal a sentence in his mind. Finally it came out, slowly but distinctly.

"In Germany," he said, "officers travel first class!"

II

Ich Bin Ein Soldat

Thu staff car waiting outside the railway station in Amsterdam was identical to that which had taken me to the station in Leeuwarden — an open Mercedes. I was ushered into the rear seat. The young guard who had accompanied me on the train sat on one side of me, and a second guard, who was with the Mercedes, sat on the other side. The driver sat in front by himself.

My imagination, which had done so much for

me during our visit to the Afsluit Dijk earlier in the day, had free rein again. I became once more the Very Important Personage, seated with my guard of honour in the official Mercedes, being feted with a tour of a great European city.

Our destination was a Wehrmacht prison somewhere in the heart of the city. When our pleasant drive through Amsterdam came to an end, I was delighted to find that the courtyard opened onto a view of a real Dutch windmill, its great blades whirling furiously just above the adjoining roofs.

I had never imagined windmills in a city. Climbing out of the car in the courtyard, I looked up at it in wonder. One of the troops standing by tried to explain what it was doing there.

"*Papier,*" he said. One of the others helped him out. "A paper mill." A windmill was only something I had seen in travelogues and schoolbooks. It belonged in the realm of Don Quixote and fairy tales. This was a real one, and was actually working. I was thrilled.

But the sunshine and excitement came to an end when I was conducted to a windowless stone dungeon and a steelplate door slammed behind me. The only light came from a single naked bulb in the ceiling and what little penetrated from a small grilled opening in the steel door. The furnishings were simple — a wooden bunk with a palliasse, a small wooden shelf extending from the wall as a table, and a stool. The stool was a small wooden disc mounted on an iron pipe pedestal.

I had never before been in a prison cell. Sitting down on the bunk, I began to recall all the boyhood stories I had read about people in dungeons. There had been tales of prisoners who made friends of birds and spiders and even rats, and did all sorts of bizarre things to save their sanity. I didn't see any spider webs.

I thought of Sir Walter Raleigh writing his *History of the World* in the Tower of London. That wasn't too cheerful a thought, for I recalled that eventually they had chopped off Raleigh's head. There had been another yarn with a happier ending, about the Count of Monte Cristo, incarcerated in the dreaded Ile d'Yf. And there was a book I had read and re-read as a boy for years: Silvio Pellico's *My Twenty Years in Prison*, the biography of one of Italy's early patriots, one of the revolutionary Carbonari. Silvio had eventually been liberated, but the thought of twenty years was a bit depressing.

For the first time in my life, I found I could really relate to Sir Walter Raleigh and Silvio Pellico and the Count of Monte Cristo and scores of other celebrated prisoners. Just thinking about them helped; I seemed to have company.

I soon found another solace. The prisoners' latrine was in another part of the complex, and one had to cross the wide courtyard to reach it. This meant a view of the great windmill en route, which became a source of joy. The German guards never complained, no matter how many times I had them escort me to the latrine. I would walk as slowly as I dared, watching the enormous flailing vanes as I walked. The guards were quite content to accommodate themselves to my pace, and I guessed that we were enjoying the windmill together.

Evenings were an even more exciting time to visit the latrine. To one side of the courtyard there was a raised patio, decked out with little tables and chairs and big fancy parasols, like a sidewalk café. Here each evening German officers would gather with their ladies, chatting to the accompaniment of clinking glasses and the restrained music of a string quartet.

And there were cigarettes.

Any prison is normally a place of rigid rules, and one of the rules here was that smoking by prisoners was strictly forbidden. I was told of this rule the very first day, when one of the guards, a young fellow with the clean, fresh look of a farm boy, asked me whether I smoked. He didn't have much English, and the query came largely through pantomime. I made him understand, with some eagerness, that I did smoke.

"Is *verboten*," he said. He made a slicing motion across his throat with one hand to suggest what could happen to a guard caught giving cigarettes to a prisoner. But once he had satisfied himself that I thoroughly understood the situation, he reached into his pocket and pushed a fresh, unopened pack of cigarettes into my hands.

There followed a further difficult exercise in communication. We discovered that both of us had been exposed to some French in high school but had forgotten it in just about the same degree. After several minutes of patient jabbering and gesturing, the guard's message was clear:

"If any officer comes along and finds the cigarettes, tell him another officer gave them to you . . . *verstehen?*"

He then showed me a clever hiding place for the cigarettes in an intricate nook in the bunk and gave me some matches and a solemn, conspiratorial wink:

"*Ich bin ein Soldat . . . Sie sind ein Soldat . . . ist der Krieg!*"

After a day or two the visits to the latrine and the windmill watching lost their novelty. Confinement began to impose its monotony. The Germans had allowed me to keep the flat package of Horlicks Malted Milk tablets that had been part of my escape kit. The tablets were about the size and shape of dominoes. I tried to pass the time pretending they were warships and manoeuvering them over the blanket on my bunk in simulated war games, but I quickly tired of it.

I craved something to read.

On the guard's next visit I broached the subject. I used all the odds and ends of German that my peacetime newspaper experience had given me: *Zeitung, Zeitschrift, Bücher, Bilderschrift.* An hour or two later the guard returned, bringing with him two magazines. One was a 1940 issue of *Yachting*; the other, a 1941 issue of *Power Boating*, both published in the United States.

I was delighted. I settled myself on my iron pipe stool, smoothed out the copy of *Yachting* on the little shelf and began to read. I read every article in the magazine and then started on *Power Boating.* When I had finished all the articles, I turned to the advertisements. All this consumed the best part of several days.

It was only after I had devoured and digested everything in both magazines that I fell back on my

newly discovered propensity for fantasy. I was no
longer the Very Important Person on my state visit
to a European capital, nor the Count of Monte
Cristo languishing in the Ile d'Yf. I had become a
millionaire with an estate on Long Island, shopping
for a luxury sailing yacht for an extended world
cruise.

But what craft of all the dozens in the magazines should I purchase? There were so many fac-
tors to be considered, and I applied myself to the
task with diligence.

There would be a shakedown cruise to the West
Indies, with a guest list of four in addition to my
wife and me. I should need plenty of room to enter-
tain. There must be a good bar and a well-stocked
wine locker. And the vessel had to be a seaworthy,
deep-sea sailer. Price, of course, was no considera-
tion. When you play such games in a prison cell,
you have all the money in the world.

I culled the magazines from cover to cover,
comparing craft with craft by one criterion after
another. The hours passed easily, and I discovered
that I was even able to worry about my yacht, lying
on my bunk, long after the Germans had switched
off the light at bedtime.

One afternoon I had just made the decision to
spurn all the advertisements and commission the
celebrated yacht designer John Alden to build me
something unique, when there was a clanging at
the door of my cell and the young German guard,
the same fellow who had given me the cigarettes,
appeared. After opening the door, he backed out into the corridor. When he reappeared a moment

later, he was holding something carefully in both hands.

The something was covered with a snow-white napkin. He stepped gingerly into my cell, set the object down on my shelf table and whipped off the napkin with a flourish.

And there it was, the most gorgeous bowl of strawberries and cream I had ever seen. The berries were huge; I swear three or four would have filled a cup. And the cream was a rich, heavy, yellowish Devonshire cream.

I tried to thank the guard but somehow couldn't make the right words come out. I just stood there returning his happy grin. And once again there was that philosophic shrug and a wry grimace as he sought to explain it all:

"Sie sind ein Soldat . . . Ich bin ein Soldat."

That explained everything; *c'est la guerre!*

III

In the Land of Der Rattenfänger

We travelled to Germany on the Amsterdam-Berlin Express, and it was one of the most memorable of all the many train journeys I have ever made. Trains had always fascinated me. My boyhood had been nurtured generously on the beautifully exciting illustrations in *Railway Magazine*, and on the train to Germany I found myself remembering never-to-be-forgotten train journeys of days gone by. There had been childhood adventures between London and Pen-

zance on the Cornish Riviera Express. Later, in
Canada, I had known fine hours on the International Limited between Montreal and Toronto, and
then spent almost half a lifetime riding the Ocean
Limited along Canada's Atlantic coast.

There had been seven days in the cell at
Amsterdam, and the novelty of sailing John
Alden's yacht was just beginning to wear off when
early one morning my young guard brought me hot
water, soap and a razor and the news that today I
should be on my way to Deutschland. A little later I
found myself in the company of a dozen other
prisoners gathered in the courtyard. They were
airmen who, like myself, had been shot down and
captured somewhere in the Netherlands during the
preceding week.

Half of them were English, officers and NCOs of
the Royal Air Force. The rest included a Czech, a
Pole, two Australians, a South African and a New
Zealander. None of us had seen each other before,
but in a sense it was a reunion. It was good to speak
one's native tongue again, exchange news, com-
pare misfortune and enjoy a prisoner's surest
solace, the fabrication of optimistic rumours.

A large motorbus was waiting in the courtyard
with engine idling. Before the Germans herded us
aboard, they distributed a day's ration of food. It
consisted of a piece of heavy, dark bread amount-
ing to about a quarter of a loaf for each man, along
with a four- or five-inch portion of spiced bacon
sausage about two inches thick.

"You'll get some coffee along the way," they
said.

"Coffee?" said one of our number dubiously.

The German laughed.

"Our kind of coffee," he said. "It's the only kind you're going to get. Haven't you heard there's a war on?"

The lack of something in which to wrap our bread and sausage would normally have seemed an atrocious hardship. But seven days in a prison cell had changed my values. There was something novel, even vaguely refreshing, about having to stow bread and sausage in one's pockets. It was as if for the great freedom I had just lost I had discovered one tiny, compensating freedom. It was like being a small boy again, free to fill my pockets with string, foxes' paws, a jackknife and a dead frog.

At the railway station we were escorted quickly through the waiting room and out onto the platform. I was surprised to find the train appearing so well groomed. War had brought a certain dowdiness to the trains back in England. But some of the carriages on this train bore little wooden plaques announcing the train's destination: Berlin. We travelled in an ordinary passenger coach, with our dozen prisoners distributed between two compartments. The guards, tommy-guns over their shoulders, took up posts in the corridor.

The coach was comfortable, the sausage was good, and there was something soothing about the way the wheels clicked over the rails. Not caring to think about the business of being shot down, I quite forgot the war. It was better to enjoy the sausage and look out the window. Sometimes there were men and women working in the fields. Along the highways we saw boys and girls pedalling their bicycles to school. There were wildflowers along the right-of-way and a bright greenness everywhere. Nowhere was there any hint of war.

My enchantment with the scenery soon gave way to a vague restlessness. I found myself looking for some sign that we were nearing the border or that we had actually passed the frontier into Germany. Through the polarization of war, Germany had become a central theme in all our lives. Now that we were her prisoners, our curiosity about this country had been heightened. The sensation was puzzling. I had no illusions; I knew that the fields would be green like other fields. But there was a mounting eagerness to be able to look out that train window and be able to say, "Now . . . now, this is Germany!"

After about a half-hour of this I got to my feet and stood in the doorway to the corridor. Two guards were chatting by the window. They looked at me expectantly. I tried a grin on them and pointed to the blurred landscape outside.

"Deutschland?" I asked.

The guards looked puzzled. One of them looked out the window, as if he had not given the matter much thought. What he saw didn't help him much. He glanced at his watch and then consulted his comrade. Both looked at their watches, conversed some more, looked out the window again, and then came to a decision.

"*Noch nicht!*"

I learned something valuable from that brief interchange. My query had an interesting effect on the guards. The fact that I had shown an interest in their country, in even so minimal a context as to whether we had reached it or not, appeared to have affected the relationship between us. A few minutes later, after I had returned to my seat in the compartment, I saw one of the guards stop the train conductor in the corridor. There was a brief referral to watches; then the guard poked his head into the compartment and beckoned to me:

"*Zehn Minuten . . . zehn . . . verstehen Sie?*"

My ignorance of German was frustrating. I shook my head. The guard held up the fingers of both hands and then pointed to his watch. I nodded.

"What the hell's that all about?" asked the Australian.

"He says its ten minutes to the German border."

"Oh, happy day," said the Australian. "What are we supposed to do? All stand to attention and sing *Deutschland über Alles*?"

There was some joking and laughter, but most of the boys checked their watches and began to show a new interest in the world beyond the windows. I had thought there might be a barricade or some kind of checkpoint at the border. There wasn't. There could have been some sort of surveyor's mark that we missed. The first knowledge we had of passing the frontier came when one of the guards, who had obviously seen what he was looking for, turned away from the window and yelled at us:

"*Deutschland . . . jetzt!*" He pointed to the

green fields beyond and laughed in an amused way, as if he were entertaining some children.

"What the hell's he laughing at?" said the Aussie. "Now we're really in the bag!"

We changed trains at Hannover. The guards explained that we were destined for Frankfurt am Main and that we should have a half-hour wait for the next train. They ushered us into a serviceman's canteen, where they produced some reasonably good ersatz coffee, and I finished off my bread and bacon sausage. After coffee we went back on the platform, and several uniformed railway employees gathered about us in curiosity. One of them strolled into our group and spoke to us in excellent English.

"Tourists, eh?"

He was smiling and seemed not at all unfriendly, proud of his English and happy to have an opportunity to parade it.

"That's right. We're tourists."

"*Ja.*" He laughed good-naturedly. "Travelling by air, too. Not so?" He pointed to our air force insignia.

"You know any better way?" said the Australian.

The German laughed again.

"It's much safer on a train. Haven't you boys found air travel a little dangerous?"

He was obviously enjoying his chat with us, and when we laughed with him he seemed more than pleased.

"So now, my friends, so now you will spend a little holiday with us in Deutschland. No?"

This didn't seem hilariously funny, but we laughed. After all, this was a better reception in Germany than many of us had expected. There had been ugly tales of Allied airmen being beaten with rifle butts, and much worse. This railwayman's gentle humour wasn't hard to take. We could well afford to laugh with him.

"Yes," I said. "A German holiday. Where did you learn your English? You speak well."

"In England. Where else? I worked there. At the Hotel Cecil in London. At the Savoy. And in Bournemouth. Ah, there's a fine place, Bournemouth. More modern. Almost American. Bournemouth was good. The money was good. All hotel work. See, that's how I come to know all about tourists. *Ach*, so. Gentlemen, I see your train."

He stepped away from us as the Frankfurt train steamed majestically into the station.

"*Wiedersehen*, gentlemen, and a happy holiday in Germany!"

But we hadn't seen the last of him. A little later, after we had boarded the train, he came strolling along the platform until he was abreast of our compartment. The window was open. He stood there a moment, and then, just a few seconds before the train began, to move, he looked in on us. The smile on his face was a little faded.

"I wish it were over, this war. Some day I want to work in England again, or go to America. Ah, well. *Wiedersehen!*"

After the train had pulled out of Hannover, it occurred to me that the only Germany I knew was the Germany of my early reading, the Germany of history and geography books and, more important, the Germany of fairy tales, poetry and Wagnerian music. The first recognizable feature of this imprinted Germany presented itself when the train stopped at Hameln.

I looked twice at the name of the station. It was printed in the characteristic bold sans serif lettering of the *Deutsche Reichsbahn.* Hameln.

Hameln. It had a familiar ring. Was this by any chance the Hamelin of our second grade readers? The town of the Pied Piper and the rats and the poor little schoolchildren enticed into a never-never land in the mountains never to be seen again? Could this really be Hamelin?

The guards might know.

But the question was more complicated than asking the distance to the German frontier. I pointed first to the sign on the station, then put my hands to my face and, wiggling all my fingers, did the best to simulate a man playing a flute. I felt a little foolish.

The guards looked at me in astonishment. So did some of the passengers who happened to be passing down the corridor. I tried harder to look like the Pied Piper and several times mouthed the words, ''Pied Piper.'' I made one more effort, this time whistling a tune as I played my imaginary flute and turning to indicate the imaginary rats behind me.

One of the guards suddenly exploded in recognition. He gave a loud laugh, slapped his thigh several times and then fairly shouted at his comrade:

"Aha! Der Rattenfänger! Der Rattenfänger!"

Germans, apparently, don't identify the Pied Piper by the name familiar to the English. To Germans he is *der Rattenfänger* — the ratcatcher.

The guards thought it a great joke. There was much laughing as they explained to curious passengers what all the commotion was about. One of the guards kept repeating to me the words *"der Rattenfänger,"* as if to make sure I would not forget them. I repeated them after him and was immensely pleased with myself. I had been on German soil only a matter of hours, and here already I knew the word for ratcatcher!

Captivity had brought an initial feeling of disorientation, a sense of sudden detachment from a familiar world. The brief stop at Hameln had cured that. A fairy tale, learned in early childhood, had suddenly become a solid fixed point in a real world. That look at the station sign had returned me to the warm security that went with the fairytale stories of childhood.

As the train slipped out of Hameln and steamed south through the valley of the Lahn, I caught sight of a great, brooding hill. That, unmistakeably, was the mountain into which the Pied Piper and the children had vanished.

I was as happy as I had ever been. I was leaning easily against the wall of the corridor, looking out the window, basking in the warm July sun and waiting for more wonders like Hameln. Germany was a land of green slopes and darker green wooded hilltops. I could relax and drink it all in even while the two guards, encouraged by my performance at

Hameln, launched me into my second lesson in German. With the aid of their fingers, they were teaching me to count.

"*Eins, zwei, drei, vier, fünf, sechs, sieben, acht, neun und zehn!*"

I glanced at my watch. It was four o'clock. At this time the previous day I had been sailing John Alden's imaginary yacht in a stone-walled cell in Amsterdam. A week earlier I had been taking tea in the officers' mess in England. Now I was learning German, from two men with tommy-guns slung over their shoulders, in the land of the Pied Piper — no, in the land of *der Rattenfänger.*

So much had happened in so short a time. I tried to put it all together, but nothing really fitted. There had been a dark sky, a subdued droning of engines, the restful greenish glow of the luminescent instrument panel, then a thundering, terrifying violence of noise and flame and a deathly silent floating through a black sky. And, after that, tulips and canals and magic windmills, and the Afsluit Dijk, and John Alden's yacht, and now the Pied Piper of Hamelin.

For the first time in my life, I was able to understand the art of Salvador Dali. The 20-millimetre cannon in a Messerschmitt 110 had projected me into the world of surrealism. I would do my best to enjoy it.

The guard hitched his gun a little higher on his shoulder and held up his hands again.

"*Sieben, acht, neun, zehn!*"

Each time he arrived at that last little finger, the *zehn* came out like a shout of triumph.

"Gut! Das ist gut!" It was good to see how much he enjoyed his pupil's progress.

That stretch of railway adventure ended at Frankfurt, where we remained for several uneventful days at the central Luftwaffe interrogation centre, Dulag Luft, situated in the quiet suburban community of Oberursel. When our odyssey resumed, we were on the train again, this time destined for the little Lower Silesian town of Sagan, where the Luftwaffe ran the principal camp for captured air force officers at Stalag Luft 3.

It was a less comfortable journey. A passenger car had been converted into a mobile prison cage by the addition of heavy barbed wire across the windows. It carried about fifty of us over the 500 kilometres to Sagan, and it was a tiresome trip of two days. Our coach was hooked to the rear of a slow freight. Time and time again we were shunted off to a siding to make way for fast passenger trains or for troop trains and fast freights. Military traffic had the right-of-way, and we saw huge cargoes of tanks, guns and trucks, all of them moving east to the Russian front.

The marshalling yards at Erfurt brought a prolonged halt, along with a brief yet welcome diversion. Our coach had been shunted onto a track spliced between two trains of cattle cars. One of our Australians, whose ranching background had given him an uncanny grasp of livestock communication, bawled out the window in a remarkably accurate simulation of a lowing cow.

The response was astonishing.

There must have been a thousand head of cattle

in the marshalling yards, and it seemed as if every last one responded to the Aussie's call. The noise was deafening. It was more cattle noise than I had heard over a lifetime. It was entertainment of the jolliest kind, and when for a moment the volume of noise seemed to subside the Australian would stoke up the decibels with more of his inimitable bawling. We were delighted with him.

One of the guards suddenly poked his head into the compartment. He appeared on the verge of panic.

"Nichts! Nichts!"

He shook his head vigorously and held up a reproving hand. All we could do was laugh. A second guard, who had some English, turned up to plead for silence.

"Please, gentlemen. You must stop. Please. It is too much!"

The Australian was enjoying himself, howling with boyish laughter when not bawling like a cow.

"It's free speech," he told the guard. "Free speech for cows!"

Everybody laughed except the Germans.

"No, no. You keep people awake. Please!"

The Australian eventually tired of his fun, and we all settled back for another few hours of fitful slumber.

There was an exceptionally long halt at Leipzig. I recalled from my old geography texts that the *Hauptbahnhof* at Leipzig was the largest and busiest railway station in Europe, and possibly in all the world, but it was nowhere to be seen.

"But this is Leipzig Süd," we were told, not the

central station. The guard went on to explain that our train was now standing in the largest marshalling yard in the world.

One of the through lines appeared to be only a track away from us, and it suddenly contributed yet another prized item in my collection of railway memories. It was the Rome-Berlin Express. The war had given this line a new status, putting it in the exalted company of such elite trains as the Orient Express, the Rayon d'Or, the Flying Scotsman and the Broadway Limited. In 1942, the Rome-Berlin Express had become the dramatic symbol of the alliance between the two principal enemy powers in Europe.

It was an impressive spectacle. Threading its way through the railway yard, the train was moving at no more than five or ten miles an hour in an aura of prestige and majesty. The locomotive retained its peacetime elegance, and the sleek, heavy, immaculately painted carriages rolled by with a subdued, well-bred click of wheel on rail. The impression was one of substance and quality. Modestly small signs bearing the legend "Rome-Berlin" flanked the doors of each car.

Passengers looked out from some of the windows. In other windows the blinds were drawn against the bright July sun. When the dining car came abreast of us, we could see that every table was occupied. The train was moving even more slowly, perhaps waiting for some war traffic to clear on the line ahead, and there was ample time to study the dining car and its occupants.

The napery was crisply white; silverware and

cut glass twinkled in the sunlight. Waiters moved effortlessly up and down the car, now leaning deferentially over a table, with attentive ear, now pouring expertly from a benapkinned bottle. It was like a splendid scene from stage or film. Once again, as at the Afsluit Dijk, I had the feeling that it was all being staged for me. It was as if the entire train had been moved into position in the Leipzig yards, complete with professional actors and actresses under the eye of some distinguished director, solely for my entertainment.

Another thought occurred to me. Only a few weeks earlier, back in Britain riding the Flying Scotsman to Edinburgh, I had been travelling under somewhat similar conditions. Now I was no longer in the dining car. I was outside, in a prison car, looking in.

One of the English airmen sitting beside me uncannily echoed my thoughts.

"Those officers," he said. "Probably on their way to join Rommel in North Africa. Who knows? A few weeks from now they could be riding in a prison car, just like us. On the other hand, they could be dead!"

As the dining car pulled out of sight behind some freight cars I had a last glimpse of a young Wehrmacht officer leaning across the table and smiling into the face of a young woman.

Then the Rome-Berlin Express was gone.

IV

A Taste of Freedom

It was my first night in Stalag Luft 3, the Luftwaffe's prison camp for captured officers of the Allied air forces. I was perched on the edge of an upper bunk in a crowded barrack room. New prisoners were always assigned upper bunks. Smoke and odours rise, and the older prisoners, by right of seniority, lived in the less polluted atmosphere of the lower bunks. So it was that I found myself sitting on the upper bunk, a little suffocated by the fug, swinging my legs and watching in bewildered wonderment what went on in the room below.

It was like a scene from a witches' Sabbath. At one end of the room, where I recalled seeing a ceramic-tiled stove a little earlier, there was a gaping square hole in the floor. The window blackouts were closed, and the electric light had been switched off by the *Kommandantur* at the appointed lights-out time. The room was lighted by smelly, flickering candles made from margarine and shoe polish. In this eerie light I watched naked and half-naked men, their bodies shiny with sweat, slipping in and out of the black hole. Some carried cloth bags, pails or old tin cans.

At the other end of the room, a dozen men, their shadows grotesque against the walls, were huddled around a table. One of them was manipulating a Ouija board. They were trying to communicate with old air force comrades whom they knew to have died in operations against the enemy.

The exercise at the black hole in the floor I could understand. The hole was clearly the entrance to what was hoped might turn out to be an escape tunnel. The Ouija board séance I found more difficult to understand. These men were all commissioned officers, educated men. They had been pilots and navigators, radio operators and flight engineers — all normally rational men. Now I found them busy with something akin to witchcraft. Obviously I had much to learn.

I found it more interesting when the man operating the Ouija board reported excitedly that he thought he had made a "contact." The others seemed sceptical. There had to be verification of identity, they said. The spirit might be an impostor, they said. There must be careful investigation.

"Operating out of Waddington, wasn't he? Forty-four Squadron? Ask him the name of that little redhead barmaid in the Snake Pit in Lincoln."

The candlelight cast a ghostly shadow over the planchette. The operator was a lanky Australian with long, bony fingers. He interrogated the contact with appropriate and gentle restraint.

"Jim, Jim . . . I say, Jim, old boy . . . are you there, Jim? Jim, do you remember the Saracen's Head in Lincoln? You know, the jolly old Snake Pit? Of course you do, old boy. Now then, Jim, we feel sure it's you, but just to be sure and certain, Jim, will you tell us the name of that barmaid in the Snake Pit? You know, the redhead. Remember her? Never mind the whole name, Jim. We haven't time. Just the initials. That's a good fellow."

The planchette squeaked across the board and the candles spluttered uneasily. At the other end of the room a huge, glistening naked figure emerged like a wraith from the blackness of the escape hatch. In one hand, he carried a table knife; in the other, a tin basin that was filled with sand. He looked like a demented figure from a Hogarth madhouse. He stopped for a moment to watch the séance and suddenly laughed loudly.

One of the spiritualists growled at him.

"Bugger off, you bastard!"

The nude figure laughed again; then his shining, sweaty body vanished down the black hole.

"Looks like the first initial is G," the Australian said. "Does that sound right?"

"No, her first name was Betty," one of the RAF men said.

"Hey you shouldn't have said that. Now you've told him what her name is."

"Jesus, if he's dead he knows that anyway, doesn't he?"

"Shush, shush," said the Australian. "Maybe poor old Jim made a mistake. Jim, Jim. Are you there, Jim? About that first name, Jim, are you sure it was G? Just say yes or no, Jim. There's a good chap!"

Two more naked figures slipped into the room and vanished without a sound into the black hole. The candles sizzled and flared and the Ouija board squealed as the planchette slid across its surface.

"Aha! It says yes. He says her name begins with a G!"

"The hell with that! Her name was Betty!"

"Yeah, but hold on a minute, mate. Betty could mean Elizabeth, and that begins with an E. And, anyway, who knows what her real name was? Half those barroom tarts make up phony names, you know that. I knew a babe in Nottingham called Mary. Then she went to work in a fancy pub up in London and called herself Casabianca. Casabianca! Can you imagine!"

"Look, lads, let's forget the barmaid," said the Australian. "Let's ask him something else, like what OTU he trained at."

"Can't do that, old boy. Breach of security."

"What the hell do you mean, breach of security? You think the Jerries got spies up there, too? Don't be ridiculous!"

"Hush up, fellows!" said the Australian. "Jim's trying to say something. It's coming through strong, real strong. I can feel it. Go on, Jim, old boy! We're listening.

The planchette was squeaking like a slate pencil. A dozen necks were stretched to watch the pointer sliding along the alphabet. Several of the group were following it in whispers.

"O...S...A...B...R...K...K..."

"But that doesn't make sense. OSABRKK. What the hell does that spell?"

"Write it down, write it down. They say the spirits are often weak so soon after passing over. Maybe he is trying to tell us something and just doesn't have the strength!"

"That's right, and I think I've got it! He's saying Osnabrück. That's it, boys! It's Osnabrück!"

"That's ridiculous! Why should he be bothered telling us the name of a German city?"

"Maybe that's where he bought it."

"But he didn't. He copped it at Wilhelmshaven. It was flak."

"Then maybe he's trying to tell us that's where tonight's raid is."

"Don't be a bloody fool! We hit Osnabrück just about every second night, anyway. That makes no sense. Try him again, cobber!"

It had been a long day and I was tired. There had been little sleep on the train. The planchette was still squeaking when I pulled off my boots, dragged a blanket over my head and went to sleep.

When I woke in the morning, the place was quiet. Peeking over the edge of the bunk, I saw that the stove was back in its proper place where last night there had been a black hole. Someone had already opened the blackouts, and the early summer sun was flooding the room. My eyes made a casual sweep of my new quarters and came to rest on a crudely lettered slogan painted across the ceiling over my head. It read:

THINK OF THE LONG, HUNGRY YEARS AHEAD.

I was spared the interrogation by the prisoners' own camp administration, to which new prisoners were subjected upon arrival. Interrogation was a precaution against the planting of an informer among us. I was immediately vouched for by several prisoners who had known me either in Canada or in Britain. In some cases newcomers had been segregated until their satisfactory knowledge of such trivia as the route names of Toronto tram lines or the state flower of Massachusetts had been accepted as proof of their bona fides.

A few days of orientation followed. There was much to be learned about the mechanics of the society into which we had been admitted. One could not ignore the subtle nuances of social status. Prisoners came to know themselves as Kriegies, after the German for prisoners of war, *Kriegsgefangenen.* There were two classes of Kriegies: Old Kriegies and New Kriegies.

The Old Kriegies assumed a certain measure of

priority and privilege. It was a privilege stemming from their degree of "antiquity," not unlike that of European aristocracy. They rated the more desirable bunks because they had arrived when the camp was new. They had experience; they were wordly-wise in the business of dealing with the Germans, in the science of scrounging, and in playing the black market and gambling in sterling. They carried themselves with an air of sophisticated sangfroid and an affectation of authority.

But there was nothing offensive about this class distinction. New Kriegies quickly recognized it for what it was, an innocent posture affected as some compensation for the burden of long captivity. And there was the warming knowledge that someday they, too, could join the ranks of the upper class, for it had become an unwritten law that the passage of one year of captivity automatically conferred upon a prisoner the exalted rank of Old Kriegie.

I was scarcely over the first few days of orientation and was still somewhat confused by it all when I received word that I was to report to the senior British officer — the SBO, the officer recognized by the German *Kommandantur* as the paramount authority within the camp and the authorized spokesman for its inmates.

The interview was brief.

The SBO was Group Captain Martin Massey, a man in his sixties who had begun his air force career in World War I. In the current war, he had received a posting to Washington to serve as liaison officer with U.S. strategic bombing personnel. He had decided, as a matter of conscience, that before going to Washington he ought to fly at least one typical bombing operation over Germany. The operation turned out to be only too typical, and he ended up in Stalag Luft 3 with the rest of us.

He came quickly to the point.

"I understand, Brown, that you were a journalist before you enlisted in the air force."

"A newspaperman, sir," I said.

"Quite so. Well, you could be useful to us here . . . help carry on the war effort, so to speak. Propaganda and all that. I'm sure you'd fit in. Wing Commander Williams is in charge of all that sort of thing. He'll explain it to you. I want you to report to Wing Commander Williams right away."

"Yes, sir."

I was immensely pleased. I left the group captain in a state of restrained excitement. My imagination, which had helped me so much during my first days of captivity, rose once more to the occasion. I thought of the black hole under the stove and had visions of some underground operations room, perhaps with a secret radio transmitter and a printing press. I had joined the air force with the secret ambition of becoming the Drake of the Skies. I had failed in that. But now I was being given a chance to be some kind of Scarlet Pimpernel, an agent in secret operations against the enemy. I was positively thrilled.

Wing Commander Taffy Williams, in addition to being chief of the information operation, was also a block commander. This entitled him to the privacy of a small cubicle at the end of the barrack block he commanded. I called on him at once and found him in.

He was seated at a table by an open window. He appeared to be busy with some kind of hobby that involved old empty jam jars, pieces of paper, scissors and other assorted odds and ends. He turned to greet me.

"Good show! You're just in time to lend me a hand. We've got a propaganda job. Something to break the morale of the civilian population, you know. Sow doubt and all that. Not much we can do at the present time, but we do have to make a start, don't we? Small beginnings, eh what? I'm sure you can be of help. We need professional people. Now let me show you . . ."

He swung back to the table and picked up one of the jam jars. An elastic band held a piece of cheesecloth over the top of the jar. As he picked it up, there was an angry humming sound.

"Bumblebees," he said, handing me the jar.

They were bumblebees, all right — about a dozen of them, all trying their best to escape.

"Oh, I have a team of the boys out collecting them. They find them over by the cookhouse and among the weeds. There's more of 'em." He pointed to two more jars on the windowsill. "Very well. Now let me show you the rest of the business."

I handed back the jar of bees, and in return he passed me a tiny slip of paper. It was almost tissue paper, not unlike the paper used for airmail letters. It was about four inches in length, and had been cut in the triangular shape of a pennant. On one side, it said DEUTSCHLAND KAPUT. On the reverse side it said, HITLER KAPUT.

The nature of our propaganda effort suddenly dawned on me. The bumblebees were to carry our devastating message to the German populace.

"I'm afraid it's the best we can do right now, old boy," said Wings. He handed me a gentleman's light leather glove for my right hand.

"Now, what we do is this. I attach this thread to the pennant, see? With a running noose at the end. Now, when I make a little opening in the jar, you'll grab the first bee that comes out.

"You'll have to be careful — gentle, you know. We mustn't hurt the little devil or he'll be no good to us, will he? You must hold him gently by the wings while I slip the noose over his backside and make it fast — but not too tight, mind you. And just where his thorax and abdomen meet. And, after that, well, the best way to begin is to begin, what?"

About an hour later, the jar was empty. One after another the bees had been pinioned and harnessed to their banners and released out the window. The wing commander was delighted to see how well they handled their burden.

"Just the right wing-loading, what? Had to figure that out. Any more weight and they couldn't maintain altitude. Thanks, old boy. That's about it for today. How about tomorrow morning, right after *Appell*?"

The bumblebee duty led to more interesting things. From my first week in the camp, I had been making the most of the standard German language textbook made available to the millions of foreign workers in the land. Practice was no problem. Fluent German speakers among the prison population were common, and we had occasional conversations with the guards. About the third or fourth month of captivity I heard from "Tim" Walenn, whom I knew to be one of the top figures in the camp's intelligence organization.

Gilbert Walenn was a London-born flight lieutenant in the Royal Air Force. I wasn't quite sure precisely what he did in the camp, but I soon found out.

"How would you like to join the staff of Dean and Dawson?" he asked.

"Dean and Dawson. Oh." I had heard the name several times around the camp. I knew what it signified. Dean and Dawson was a familiar British travel agency, like Cook's. The name was used among prisoners as a code for that branch of the escape organization that provided the identity cards, labour permits and other forged documents needed to give escaping prisoners some suitably authentic cover.

"It's a big job," he said. "I want someone to build me a card index system, with a card for just about every city and town in the Reich. You know, the name of the *Polizeipräsident*, the chief of police, the correct address of the *Reichsarbeitsdienst*, the local labour recruiting centre, addresses of the principal industries — all that sort of thing. It's the kind of information we need to have quickly available, and it has to be accurate — the right names and the right addresses."

"How do we get that sort of thing?" I asked.

"Most of it from the daily newspapers," Tim said. "A lot of it from the classified ads. In the help-wanted columns, in the labour recruitment ads. We need good addresses of industrial firms. And we need names, names of real people. You'll find them in the news columns, even in the obituaries. Look, I'll show you what I mean."

He pulled a little notebook from his jacket pocket and extracted from it a small newspaper clipping. It was the typical black-bordered obituary notice for a Hans Schmidt, a young German soldier who had died the *Heldentod* for *Führer und Vaterland* on the Russian front.

"Look at this," said Tim. "Poor Hans came from a good family. See? Survived by his father, Otto Schmidt, *Polizeipräsident* Liegnitz . . . That's the kind of information we need. If we provide an escaper with travel papers purporting to be okayed by the Liegnitz police we want the authentic name of the *Polizeipräsident*. Get it?

"I'll get you all the daily newspapers, and I'll get you some cards, and you can go to work. You'll make an entry on everything you think will help to get an escaper from A to B. We've got people who can do all the paperwork and forging. What we need is authentic information."

Tim Walenn, I discovered, was chief of the camp's forgery department. He had a small group of assistants, and it was a joy working with them. It was arranged that I would live with them in their mess so that while I pored over the classified ads in the *Völkischer Beobachter* and the *Frankfurter Zeitung* I could occasionally relax by watching

Gordon Brettell use a piece of razor blade to delicately carve the logo for a police department stamp out of a Canadian YMCA hockey puck.

Gordon Brettell was typical of the artisans in Walenn's forgery studio. He was a British public-school boy, whose education had seen him through Cheltenham and Cambridge and on to the Royal Air Force, with a brief peacetime interlude driving at the Brooklands race track. He had flown Spitfires out of Biggin Hill during the Battle of Britain and later was shot down during a sweep over the French coast. His crippled Spit had nosed into an apple orchard. He had broken both legs, an arm and several ribs.

The Germans had put him in the local hospital at Abbeville. "They had a guard on the floor, but there was little chance of my running away on two broken legs. The French nurses were more than kind to me. Affectionate, really. Amazing what you can do with two broken legs, with a little help. Who'd want to run away?"

Another British public-school boy in this group was Tony Hayter, whose flair for penmanship approached genius. He worked alongside Henri Picard, a Belgian who had already won the Croix de Guerre by the time he was shot down. Picard was an artist with so sharp an eye and steady a hand that he could make a facsimile of a typewritten letter with nothing more than a mapping pen.

Arnost Valenta, a professional officer from the Czech service, was an authority on the subleties of European travel security. He was a Staff College graduate and had served on exchange programs with both the German and the Russian forces. He was a gifted linguist and scholar; he had been the first to translate Shaw's *Saint Joan* into Czech.

Albert Hake, an Australian, manufactured magnetic compasses for us. Romas Marcinkus, a Lithuanian in the Royal Air Force, had an encyclopedic knowledge of the varied escape routes across Europe. No travel papers were complete until they had the approval of Marcinkus.

The winter of 1942–43 brought the prisoners in Stalag Luft 3 their first encouraging news of the progress of the war. In November British forces had thrown Rommel back from Egypt, and the Anglo-Americans had landed in force in North Africa. In the Soviet Union the Red Army had launched its historic offensive at Stalingrad, and February had brought the surrender of the beleaguered German Sixth Army.

For Gordon Brettell and me, who by now had spent long months labouring in Tim Walenn's forgery shop, the winter brought an itch to play a more active role in the escape business. The time had come, we felt, to embark on the escape adventure for ourselves.

The Escape Committee, whose sanction was necessary, gave us its blessing and authorized what assistance we would need. Our command of German, weak as it was, could qualify us as Bulgarian immigrants, two of the many millions of foreign workers now employed in the German war industry.

Our travel papers would identify us as steelworkers. It was Romas Marcinkus who determined that we should be Bulgarians.

"Your German is atrocious — so bad, in fact, that Germans will easily believe you are Bulgarians. Germans don't think much of Bulgarians — they wouldn't expect any Bulgarian to be capable of learning another language. And you have nothing to worry about; nobody is ever going to challenge you in your native tongue. There isn't one man in a thousand in Germany who can speak or understand Bulgarian."

I had the feeling Marcinkus didn't much care for Bulgarians either.

"Why, you even look a little Bulgarian. By all means, it's your best bet. Be Bulgarians!"

Our identity papers were the best the section could produce. My alias was Goleb Plasov, steelworker from the rolling mill of the *Vereinigte Stahlwerke* in Liegnitz. My father was Jakov Plasov, my mother's given name was Natasha, and I had been born in the little village of Latulia north of Sofia. I had come to Germany after reading a *Reichsarbeitsdienst* advertisement in a Sofia newspaper. My cover papers also indicated that I was in the process of transferring from the Liegnitz plant to a new steelworks in Strasbourg. That was explained in a formal statement on *Arbeitsdienst* stationery, which also bore the stamp and signature of the Liegnitz chief of police. I was proud of that last part, since it stemmed from information gleaned during my work on the card index system.

Our exit from the camp was quite uneventful.

A new compound to house the daily increasing number of air force prisoners was under construction adjoining our own. A number of other-ranks prisoners were being employed on the project. Since under the terms of the Geneva Convention officers could not be made to work, Gordon and I changed places with two members of a working party. While the attention of escorting guards was diverted by a complicated black market cigarette transaction, we slipped away.

Since the new compound was as yet unguarded, the Germans, who had noticed our absence within minutes, assumed that we had simply walked out the main gate, and at once the hue and cry was raised throughout the entire neighbourhood. Rather cleverly, we thought, we had remained in the compound, snuggled down under a heap of new wood-shaving mattresses. Long hours later, under cover of darkness, we climbed the new and not-yet-guarded wire and vanished into the surrounding forest.

We had been outfitted in civilian clothes of a suitably proletarian cut, and in addition to our identity papers and other covering documents we carried ample German currency and pocketfuls of nourishing escape rations sufficient to last for several days. These last were candy-bar-shaped nuggets of a mixture of chocolate, raisins, nuts, milk powder and sugar, all boiled together and left to set in moulds. We also had in our heads the memorized addresses of two members of the French Resistance. One was a hotelkeeper in

Mülhausen; the other, a nursing sister in a Catholic hospital in Strasbourg.

I have never known the pure, sweet joy of living, tempered so deliciously with the sense of danger, as I knew it during the four days that elapsed between our escape and recapture. Escapers have invariably sought to characterize their escape as a matter of service duty; an officer was expected to make every effort to rejoin his unit. The truth is that escape had all the exhilarating fascination of a spine-tingling sport, and it was this aspect more than any other that beckoned to captives from the free side of the wire.

The first night, steering by stars and compass, we made a sly, backtracking circuit through heavily wooded country to the south of the camp. Our immediate destination was the little town of Sorau, about ten miles from Sagan, where we planned to catch a train for the west. The night was sharp and clear and cold, and the straight, giant German firs, in sharp silhouette against a starry sky, conjured up vignettes from Grimm's fairy tales.

Twice we hid in the brush at the side of the narrow wood-hauling road while police patrols on bicycles wheeled quietly by. The quiet of the night was broken only by a distant solemn rumbling of bombs far away to the west of us.

It was the end of March 1943, and the next day turned cold. We continued our circuitous route through the woodlands and that night took shelter in the cabin atop a forest fire lookout tower. On the following morning we emerged from the woods and took to a secondary highway that led us into the town of Sorau, whence we intended to continue our journey by train.

We found the railway station.

We now faced the first test of the authenticity of our impersonation. We were nervous as we approached the ticket window and asked for one-way, third-class tickets to Kottbus.

"Bitte . . . Kottbus . . . dritte Klasse . . . einmal."

We walked out onto the platform with the tickets in our hands. We were quietly jubilant.

Kottbus was not far distant, no more than about fifty kilometres. We had been carefully briefed about German train travel and warned never to board a *D-Zug*, or through train, since these were regularly boarded by police at checkpoints. It was much safer to travel by *Personenzug*, the local and commuter trains that stopped at every station. They were rarely checked by police.

We detrained at Kottbus, sought out the station restaurant, made a meal of unrationed soup and a stein of beer, and caught a later *Personenzug* for Leipzig.

There was a stimulating release of adrenalin when five or six German soldiers joined us in our third-class compartment. They chatted quietly among themselves until at a station along the way another soldier joined us. He was not dressed in the olive-green worn by the others but was turned out instead in the smart, sand-coloured drill of the Afrika Korps. He wore on his arm the brassard of the SS Hermann Göring Division.

The openly envious glances he received from

the other run-of-the-mill soldiery were not lost on him. There was no mistaking his pride in his special status. He positively glowed when one of them drew attention to the unusually tailored pockets of the Afrika Korps desert uniform. In no time at all he was describing his superlative equipment, telling them of the glories of his distinguished division.

He then went on to relate that his division had been resting up in garrison duty at L'orient on the French Atlantic coast but that it was now being posted to the front to face the Anglo-Americans in Tunisia. He was on his way to rejoin the division in Rome.

Behind our copy of the *Völkischer Beobachter*, which we had bought from the newsstand at Kottbus, Gordon and I listened with great interest. We were highly amused, since we were facing a big coloured poster that draped one wall of the compartment. It depicted two soldiers chatting in a railway train. By their side, an evil-looking civilian, ostensibly buried in his newspaper, exactly as we were, cocked a grotesquely oversized ear in their direction. The caption on the poster read:

Beware the Third Person!
The Enemy has Ears!

Gordon rustled the newspaper and leaned closer to me as if to point out something of interest.

"How I'd love to tap that fellow on the knee," he whispered, "and say, 'Be careful, old boy; for all you know we might be British officers!' "

Recapture is as bitter as escape is sweet. We

had changed trains at Leipzig and had arrived in Chemnitz in the early evening. We had been much encouraged by our facility in buying tickets and felt quite at ease when we joined the queue in front of the ticket window in the Chemnitz *Bahnhof* and asked for tickets to Nürnberg.

The girl at the window shook her head.

I repeated my request, with what I hoped was a better German enunciation, but she merely shook her head more vigorously. She spoke so fast that I could not make out what was amiss.

It was at this point that a policeman intervened. He seemed to have been detailed for general duty in the waiting room. He was a pleasant-looking, rather elderly man who didn't appear to be at all hostile. He asked where we wanted to go. We said we were on our way to Strasbourg. We took out our papers and told him we were going to new jobs in the steel plant at Strasbourg.

His reaction astounded us. For the benefit of all those within earshot he began to voice a bitter complaint about the Reich employment service, the *Arbeitsdienst.* Our German was good enough to catch the drift of what he was saying.

"It's a scandal! They get all these poor Italians and Slovaks and Bulgarians in the country and let them wander around like lost sheep! They don't know where they are going. Here's two more. Look at them! Bulgarians. Steelworkers. And nobody had sense enough to tell them how to get to Strasbourg!"

His little speech over, he took us aside.

"You can't travel to Nürnberg," he said. "It's

verboten. For two nights they have had big bombing there. All travel to Nürnberg is *verboten.* British terror bombers. You'd best go back to Leipzig; then get a ticket on the through train to Strasbourg. Look, give me your money. I'll get your tickets for you."

We were dazed. A German policeman was actually helping us. I handed him some money. He was still complaining about the *Arbeitsdienst* to the girl at the wicket as he bought the tickets. He handed me the tickets and some change.

"Go wait in the restaurant. Have a beer."

It would be several hours to the next train for Leipzig, he said, but he would call us when the time came. We thanked him profusely and set out for the restaurant.

"It's a bloody miracle," said Gordon, after we had ordered the beer. "I can't believe it. Our papers must be pretty convincing."

Quite late in the evening, while we were still in the restaurant, the air raid alarm sounded. Along with the other travellers in the station, we trudged down the flights of stairs to the *Luftschutzkeller.*

It was here that for the first time we began to feel self-conscious. The shelter was cramped, and we were packed in tightly with the others, so close that I felt sure some sharp eyes would notice the amateurish needlework that had transformed our bed blankets into civilian suits, or take stock of the British army boots provided us through the International Red Cross.

About an hour later the all-clear sounded, and we returned to the station restaurant and ordered another beer. After the nervous interlude in the confined quarters of the air raid shelter our confidence returned.

Then it happened.

The swinging doors of the restaurant swept open and two uniformed men entered. Their eyes scanned the room and then zeroed in on us. One of them pointed at us and said something terse to the other. The pair of them closed in. They were young men, and they were police.

Nothing was said as they escorted us downstairs and into the office and orderly room of the *Reichsbahnpolizei*, the railway police. They were not inconsiderate; they pointed us into chairs facing a long table. A moment or two later a man in civilian dress emerged from an inner office. He was smoking a cigar. He looked at us carefully for a moment and then spoke to us in French.

We produced our papers.

"Wir sind bulgarische," I said. *"Stahlarbeiter."*

"Ah, so?" He sat down at the table facing us and flattened out our papers the better to examine them. *"Aus Liegnitz, ja?"*

"Jawohl, mein Herr, aus Liegnitz," we repeated. *"In dem Walzwerk."* It would help to be a little technical and let him know we worked in the rolling mill.

He studied the documents some more and then gathered them up and returned to his office. He closed the door. We could see him through the glass partition. He had picked up the telephone. My heart sank a little. We had good papers, but how long would they stand up? What if he called the rolling mill in Liegnitz?

He emerged from his office smiling about ten minutes later. He looked over at the two policemen who had brought us in and laughed.

"*Nicht bulgarische,*" he said. "*Französisch!*"

He beckoned the pair over to the table and handed them the identity papers he had taken from us. Then he went back to his office and fetched a magnifying glass. For several minutes the three of them examined the papers carefully. In spite of our predicament, we couldn't help feeling good at the way they shook their heads in admiration of our forgeries.

"*Wunderbar! Wunderbar!*"

The civilian finally turned to us. He told us point blank we were French prisoners of war trying to get back to France. We shook our heads vigorously. We insisted there was a mistake. We were Bulgarian steelworkers. At that point he laughed again.

"*Es gibt kein Stahlwerk in Liegnitz,*" he said, "*und kein Walzwerk.*" There was nothing but a sales bureau of the *Vereinigte Stahlwerke* in Liegnitz. I felt badly about that; the misinformation was the result of my own card index work.

He lapsed again into French, and we caught the word *Gestapo*. It was quite clear that our bluff had been called, and I turned to Gordon.

"Might as well show them our dog tags," I said. Against such an emergency, as proof that we were military personnel and entitled to the protection of the Geneva Convention, we had concealed our air force identity tags in the heel of our boots. The police boss watched with interest as we each removed one of our boots. When I pointed to the heel, he obligingly produced his pocketknife. I pried off the heel and handed him the dog tags. Gordon added his.

The police boss studied the tags briefly and smiled broadly.

"Ach, so. Britische Offizieren!"

The two others showed surprise, but it was nothing like the surprise of yet another policeman who at that moment had entered the room. It was none other than the elderly kindly fellow who had purchased the tickets to Leipzig for us. He looked at us blankly for a moment and then turned to his superior.

"Bulgarische Stahlarbeiter," he said.

The others roared in laughter.

"Zwei britische Offiziere!" thundered the boss man.

The unhappy fellow paled a little and then reddened in resentment. We didn't catch every word he said, but the meaning was clear.

"And after all I did to help you," he was saying. Somehow he actually made me feel a bit of an ingrate. He had been so good to us, and now he was in trouble for it. It didn't seem just.

We were locked up in a tiny cell adjoining the police office in the station, and the next morning two police, armed with tommy-guns, escorted us through the streets of Chemnitz to the headquarters of the local Gestapo.

Now came the strangest surprise of all. We

were ushered into an office that was nothing short of palatial. It had all the Hollywood trimmings — potted palms and rubber plants, deep piled carpet, period piece furnishings. Elegance was stamped all over the place. From behind a huge desk littered with a battery of telephones a quite handsome man of middle age looked us over with a show of interest. He was smoking a cigar. I thought it surprising that he was in civilian dress.

He questioned us in good English, and it quickly became clear that he was interested primarily in where we had been and what we had been doing in the nearly four days we had been at large. He had already been in contact with the security officer "back home" at Stalag Luft 3. He knew a lot about our camp.

We were careful with our answers. Espionage and sabotage lurked behind every question. He produced a map and railway timetables, asked us to state exactly what trains we had used and at what times, what we had done between trains and what we had seen en route. Since we could see no point in doing otherwise, we told a reasonably straightforward story of our peregrinations.

After a spell of this sort of interrogation, he picked up the phone and rattled off a brief order. A short time later a series of German Army personnel, of different ranks, entered the room, came to attention and left, one after another. As each entered and came to attention, we were asked to look at his rank badges and identify them.

We passed with flying colours.

"Feldwebel. Leutnant. Gefreite."

We had been in Germany long enough to know the German ranks as well as our own. The purpose of this pantomime was not clear, unless it was to establish that we were indeed authentic military personnel. When it was over our interrogator seemed to relax a little.

"You come from a Luftwaffe camp," he said. "I hear it is quite a good camp. Is it?"

We told him that we understood it was better than most prison camps in Germany.

"And you get Red Cross food parcels there?"

Indeed, we did.

"I hear you have a library there, and a theatre, too. Not like most prison camps. You are lucky. Tell me, why did you want to escape?"

We gave him the stock answer: "It's an officer's duty, *mein Herr.*"

At that he smiled, blew a little ring of cigar smoke in our direction and leaned towards us over his big desk.

"Let me tell you something. In the first war, in 1917, I was a prisoner, too, in France. I, too, escaped from the prison camp. But I had better luck than you fellows. I got back to Germany and my regiment. Wait a moment."

He left the office and returned in a minute or two with another man, of about his own age, who was also in civilian dress. He introduced him by name.

"This man," he said, putting an arm around the other's shoulder, "was my comrade in that prison camp in France. He, too, escaped. But he was like you. They caught him and sent him back."

We chatted for a few minutes about prison camp, and I had the impression that both of them were enjoying the experience. Then he called for the two armed guards who had been standing by the door.

"You are lucky boys," he said. "You are going back to your old camp." As we turned and headed for the door, he waved his cigar at us. "Better luck next time, boys!"

We were both breathing easier as the guards led us out into the street.

"That chap," said Gordon, "must be the only decent Gestapo man who ever lived!"

V

Recaptured

I celebrated my thirty-second birthday in the little village of Grosshartmannsdorf in German Saxony. I should never have known if such a place existed had it not been for our ill-starred escape attempt. Somehow it happened that instead of being shipped directly back to Stalag Luft 3 we were sidetracked into the most dismal incarceration we had yet experienced. An old and disused factory building in Grosshartmannsdorf, a four-storey monument to nineteenth-century industry, had been converted into a barracks to house French and Russian prisoner work gangs — Germany's slave labourers.

On the fourth floor, in the dormers, there were solitary confinement cells, and we were confined in one. It was far from Waldorf luxury. The cell measured about eight feet by six feet, with a plank platform for a bed, a wooden block for a pillow and two rough, brown blankets. There was no other "furniture." It obviously served as a punishment cell for recalcitrant labourers. The barbed wire over the tiny dormer window was quite unnecessary. The window opened onto a sheer, four-storey drop to the street below.

That first night in Grosshartmannsdorf we were uncomfortable and restless. But came the dawn and I suddenly remembered that it was April the first, my birthday. Apart from the clothes I was wearing, it was about the only thing I could call my own.

Around breakfast time a guard opened the door to bring us our ration of black bread and mint tea. He was a middle-aged man, probably considered too old for active front-line service. He told us he came from Hamburg and wanted to know how long we thought the war would last. We had a pleasant chat, during which I took the opportunity to tell him that this was one hell of a way for a man to spend his birthday.

He laughed at the joke, and I thought that was the end of it. About an hour later, however, he was back again. He had with him two men in rather dirty United States Army uniforms. I suddenly recalled seeing them huddled in the Gestapo office in Chemnitz the day before. The guard, with a conspiratorial grin, explained that the Americans might join us in the cell and remain for the day. It was, he said, his birthday present for me.

He went so far as to shake my hand and wish me a happy birthday. He seemed delighted with his role as host.

The two Yanks were about as unlikely a couple as I had ever seen. One was a lieutenant, scion of a patrician family living in Scarsdale, New York. There was a lanky grace about him; he was a graduate of Princeton and spoke excellent German. His buddy was an enlisted man, private first class, a former New York City policeman of Italian stock, who spoke only Italian and Brooklynese.

They were an engaging and entertaining pair, with an almost incredible story to tell. They had been captured during the Kasserine Pass operation in North Africa and had jumped from a moving prison train in Germany in an abortive escape attempt. Both bore some superficial scratches and bruises on hands and face.

"I figured we were still in southern Germany somewhere," the lieutenant said, "and thought we might have a chance to sneak into Switzerland. We didn't have a map — well, except for this one."

He laughed and drew from his pocket a tiny notebook with a black leatherette cover, one of those calendar diaries that insurance companies and the like give their clients as souvenirs. In the centre pages was a series of coloured maps of almost microscopic projection. The whole of

Europe was encompassed on a two-by-three-inch page.

"About all I could get from that was that if we walked in a southerly direction we just might bump into the Swiss frontier. Well, it was worth a try."

They had made no attempt at concealment.

"We saw a farmer working in a field, so I went up to him and asked him which way was Switzerland. He seemed dumbfounded. He finally pointed to some hills in the distance and said he had always thought Switzerland was over there somewhere. He just kept staring after us until we were out of sight."

A little later they had been walking boldly along a paved secondary highway, making good time in their progress south, when a motorcycle policeman came in sight.

"When he slowed to a halt alongside us I figured this was the end of the line for sure. After all, we were in our U.S. Army uniforms, although we had ripped off our rank badges and our tunics were pretty dirty. Anyway, he looked us up and down and then began to give us a real tongue-lashing."

At this point in the story the Brooklynese Italian interjected.

"I don't know no German, see? I didn't know what he was saying. But by the way he was shouting at us I figured he didn't like us much. Jeez, I was wondering if maybe he was going to shoot us then and there!"

They were both laughing now.

"I couldn't believe my ears," the lieutenant said. "He must have figured we were some of those

foreign workmen, like the French and the Yugo-
slavs. He said if we wanted to keep working in Germany we'd better start behaving like Germans and
obey the rules. And we ought to know better than
to walk on the wrong side of the highway! I told him
I was very sorry, and we would remember that, and
he revved up the bike and took off."

Their freedom was shortlived. Hungry, they
had liberated a rabbit from a farmer's hutch. A little
later, after finding shelter in a railwaymen's shack
alongside the tracks, they were in the process of
stoking up the stove for a rabbit dinner when they
were apprehended by railway police.

But my birthday party was not over yet.

That evening, our Americans still with us, the
guard from Hamburg rattled his keys again and
brought some more guests for the party. They were
four French prisoners from the floor below. And
they came bearing gifts — cakes, cookies and
cigarettes. The guard brought along extra rations
of chickory "coffee" in big, steaming metal
canisters.

It was a night to remember. We were all squat-
ted on the floor on our haunches, squeezed into the
tiny cell elbow to elbow, suffocating from the deadly
Gauloises cigarettes our French friends had
brought. Every half-hour or so our Hamburg guard,
sometimes with a smirking comrade in tow, would
drop in, and we would all be joined — British,
French, American and German alike — in a dis-
daining indifference to the war that divided us and
by a hearty dedication to squeezing a little fun out
of life.

It was late that night when the guards took our

guests away to their respective cells. The heavy door clanged shut. Gordon and I stretched out on our wooden planks to sleep and dream it all over again. My thirty-second birthday party was over. It was, I think, the finest I have ever known.

The prison in Grosshartmannsdorf was a remarkable place. It was the scene not only of my most memorable birthday party but also of the most luxurious shave and haircut I have ever known. We had been in the little punishment cell under the eaves for several days, the guards explaining that they were waiting for personnel from Stalag Luft 3 to come and collect us, when it occurred to me that I was badly in need of a haircut. I assumed there was some arrangement for prisoners here to be occasionally clipped. Most of them appeared to have crew cuts.

I asked our Hamburg friend about it. There was no difficulty, he said. He would arrange it. He was back in a few minutes. He would take me to the barber now.

On the way down the stairs to the main floor, I had a good look into the living quarters of the French and Russian prisoners. Each floor was packed almost solidly with the standard three-tier bunks, but screens of meshed wire segregated one part of each floor from the others. The atmosphere was one of the utmost dismal misery, accented by a heavy stink of sweat and stale tobacco.

The "barbershop," I imagined, would likely match the rest of the place. At best, it might be like the facility back at Stalag Luft 3, where one sat on a wooden soapbox while one of the enlisted men hacked off the hair with a pair of ancient, blunt scissors.

"*Hier,*" said the guard, opening a door and waving me into the barbershop.

But I didn't move. I couldn't take a step. I stood transfixed by what I saw. I wondered if perhaps the events of the past few days, the escape and the Gestapo and the birthday party, had been too much for my mind. Was I becoming unhinged? Was I hallucinating?

For I stood on the threshold of the most elegantly equipped gentlemen's barbershop I had ever seen. What passed for the barbershop at the Royal York Hotel in Toronto would pale by comparison.

There were three standard barber chairs in a large, high-ceilinged, brilliantly lighted room that glistened with porcelained tile and chromed fixtures. Huge mirrors framed in gold covering opposing walls made the room seem even larger. The chairs faced a rank of marble sinks, and the shelves were festooned with every imaginable hairdressing aid, lotions and perfumes. Standing in wait were the two barbers, quite splendid in well-pressed uniforms of immaculate white.

Speechless, I sank into a chair.

Eventually, as my barber applied himself expertly to the shearing, I learned the story of the barbershop. It was one more of the bizarre, Alice-in-Wonderland tales that cropped up so often in my years of German captivity. With our mutual slender grasp of German, and what little remained of my high school French, my *Barbier* explained it all.

"It all comes from Occupied France," he said, his wave of hand embracing our surroundings. "You see, prisoners from occupied lands can get many things from home. There's this rich man back in Paris — he wanted to do something for the French prisoners here, and the Germans let him put in this barbershop. He paid for it all, and keeps it supplied. All very nice, *n'est ce pas?*"

After he had cut my hair he gave me a shave, and when he asked if I like a mud-pack facial massage I assented cheerfully. It might be a long, long time before I should again have pampering attention like this.

"The Germans like this idea?" I asked.

He laughed.

"Mais oui! The *Kommandant,* the office staff and all their friends — they all come here. They get their haircuts and shaves for nothing. And better than any haircut they'd get in Grosshartmannsdorf. To be sure, nobody's going to take this away!"

We left Grosshartmannsdorf the following morning. Two Luftwaffe NCOs arrived to escort us back to Stalag Luft 3. Before we left we were given our ration for the train journey. It was the same fare as I had received almost a year ago at Amsterdam — about half a loaf of bread and a good length of spiced sausage. As at Amsterdam, neither item was wrapped, and as the portions were a little more generous and a trifle too large to fit into our pockets, we had to carry them in our hands. But we had no other luggage; it was no great hardship.

Once we were on board the train, this situation improved. The railway system was one of the few sectors of the German economy into which women, in any significant numbers, had been drawn into the war effort. Apart from the engineering staff, the train crew was entirely female. Two of them, smartly uniformed young women, joined the guards and us in our compartment.

They noticed at once the bread and sausage we were holding. Their reaction reminded me of the kindly policeman in the *Bahnhof* at Chemnitz. They showed great indignation and began to scold the two guards.

The guards shrugged their shoulders and said it wasn't their fault. The guilty ones were back at Grosshartmannsdorf, they said.

One of the young women left the compartment and returned a few minutes later with some folded sheets of waxed paper. She took our rations and carefully wrapped each piece in paper and slipped an elastic band around it.

The women remained with us, chatting pleasantly about everything in the world except the war until the train rolled into Dresden station and they departed to their respective duties.

I was feeling rather good about it all. We hadn't escaped, it was true. Our mission had failed. But we had succeeded in finding a little excitement in breaking the monotony of camp life. And we had met some interesting people. There had been the nice policeman who helped us at Chemnitz, and the miraculously friendly Gestapo boss. And I had had a birthday party, and visited a magic barbershop, and two nice girls had wrapped up our bread and sausage for us.

I was still in Germany, and still a prisoner, but sitting back by the train window and watching the trees slip by I found myself quite happy.

On arrival back in Sagan there was the expected customary fifteen days of solitary confinement as punishment for trying to escape. It was what the Germans called sharp arrest, but it was in fact not too onerous. Prisoners in solitary were permitted to have books from the camp library. Our library had been furnished by the famous Bodleian Library of Oxford University and was well stocked. I sent for all five volumes of Macaulay's *History of England*; I felt it was time I made up for failing to read it during my school days.

Gordon Brettell used the quiet of solitary confinement to write some verse to commemorate our escape attempt. It was a paraphrasing of Rudyard Kipling's familiar poem, "If." It went like this:

> *If you can quit the compound undetected*
> *And clear your tracks, nor leave the smallest*
> *trace,*
> *And follow out the program you've selected,*
> *Nor lose your grasp of distance, time and*
> *space . . .*

> *If you can walk at night by compass bearing,*
> *Or ride the railways in the light of day,*
> *And temper your elusiveness with daring,*
> *Trusting that sometimes bluff will find a*
> *way . . .*

> *If you can swallow sudden, sour frustration,*
> *And gaze unmoved at failure's ugly shape,*
> *Remembering, as further inspiration,*
> *It was, and is, your duty to escape . . .*

If you can keep the great Gestapo guessing,
  With explanations only partly true,
And leave them, in their heart of hearts,
      confessing
    They didn't get the whole truth out of you . . .

If you can use your "cooler" fortnight clearly
  For planning methods wiser than before,
And treat your first miscalculations merely
    As hints let fall by Fate to teach you more . . .

If you scheme on, with patience and precision
  — It wasn't in a day they builded Rome —
And make escape your single sole ambition,
    The next time you attempt it — you'll get
      home!

Almost exactly a year later, in the Great Escape of March 1944, Gordon Brettell did attempt it again. But he didn't get home. He was recaptured near Danzig several days later and was among the fifty Stalag Luft 3 officers murdered by the Gestapo on the express orders of Adolf Hitler.

Six other members of the Dean and Dawson forgery team died with him: Walenn, Valenta, Marcinkus, Hayter, Hake and Picard.

VI

Commanders and Captives

The Allied officers in Stalag Luft 3 were lucky to have had a Prussian aristocrat, instead of some Nazi bullyboy, as their *Kommandant*. Ours was no less than a baron, *Oberst* (Colonel) Freiherr Franz von Lindeiner-Wildau. He was a man in his sixties, veteran from an elite cavalry regiment of World War I. He was a handsome figure and carried himself with the dignified stance he might have worn at the old kaiser's court at Potsdam.

Before coming to Sagan as *Kommandant* of Stalag Luft 3, he had been on the personal staff of the Luftwaffe supreme commander and the *Reichsmarschall*, Hermann Göring, and had attended him during the period of the Battle of Britain, when Göring's headquarters had been in his headquarters train, Asia, on the north coast of France.

Von Lindeiner, as we called him, was close to retirement, and it was no secret that he nursed the ambition to retire with the rank — and the pay — of a general. Our knowledge of that aspiration was one of the winning cards we held when the *Kommandant* sent for our senior officers one morning and sought to make a deal. The other high card in our hand that day had to do with the camp garbage, which went for pig swill.

The *Kommandant* had a problem.

A serious complaint had been lodged with headquarters in Berlin. There had been a mysterious epidemic in the pig population in the farm area adjoining the prison camp. One farmer after another had reported that his pigs were dying for no apparent reason. Local veterinarians had eventually come up with the answer: The pigs had been killed by ingesting pieces of broken razor blades in the swill they ate — and the swill had been coming from Stalag Luft 3.

The *Kommandant*, of course, knew very well how and why the bits of razor blades got into the swill. He didn't shout and scream about it. He accepted that the prisoners derived some satisfaction from the thought that they could still continue their war effort through little acts of sabotage. Killing

German hogs would aggravate the already tight food situation in the Reich.

"But it has to stop," he said. The high command took a grave view of sabotage, and there could be rough reprisals. Sometime in the next week or two, he went on, the inspector-general of prison camps was due to visit Stalag Luft 3. The subject of the murdered pigs would be high on the agenda, and the *Kommandant* would very much like to be able to inform the inspector-general that the practice had ceased.

Wing Commander Harry Day, RAF, was spokesman for the group in the *Kommandant*'s office. He, too, was a professional soldier, scion of an aristocratic English family and, like the *Kommandant*, a veteran of World War I. At the age of sixteen, a middy Royal Marine on HMS *Britannia*, he had won the Albert Medal for bravery under fire in the rescue of fellow crewmen trapped in a blazing gun turret.

"Wings" didn't bother to deny the allegations about the razor blades.

"But you know, *Oberst*, there really isn't that much swill leaving the camp — little but a few potato peelings, really. Now, if we had a supply of good, fresh green vegetables — you know, carrots and cabbage and beets and the like — well, there'd be a lot more swill for the pigs. Give us some issues of fresh vegetables and there'll be no more razor blades in the swill."

The *Kommandant* brightened.

"I'm glad you see it that way," he said. He would make arrangements with the commissary people at once to augment our diet with fresh vegetables. He would start the trucks rolling in the next day or two.

"The inspector-general is coming soon," he said, affecting a somewhat pained grimace as he spoke. Then he looked hard at Wings and smiled. They were both professional soldiers; they would understand each other. The *Kommandant* would guess that Wings would sympathize with his concern about promotion.

"Perhaps your boys could put on a good parade for him," he said. He thought it might be nice if just for once the prisoners turned out for *Appell* in smart formation, instead of straggling onto the parade square like a nondescript mob of derelicts. It just might make all the difference between his retiring as a half-pay colonel and getting a general's pension.

Wings frowned.

"That might not be too easy, *Oberst*. The boys are hardly in the mood for spit and polish. They haven't the gumption for any heel clicking. Some of them are so slack they can barely salute properly. What they need, *Oberst*, is some red meat in their diet, something to put 'em on their feet, give 'em some get-up-and-go! Yes, indeed, a little red meat and you've got yourself a parade!"

The day the inspector-general arrived, we were drawn up in squadron formation on the parade ground. It looked something like graduation day at West Point or RMC, and when twelve hundred pairs of heels clicked in awesome unison, the German general and his aides were visibly stunned. The

Kommandant, for his part, did his best to convey the impression that, thanks to his gifts of leadership and command, that's the way things went every day.

Over the ensuing months, we ate better than we had since any of us had arrived in camp, and it added even further to the admiration and respect we had for Wing Commander Harry Day. He was a man of the most magical and irresistible kind of charm, which was perhaps the strongest facet of his capacity for leadership. Wings had been a bit of a legend in the Royal Air Force long before the outbreak of war; older RAF prisoners spoke in hushed tones about his skill as an aerobatic pilot.

We had learned from them, too, that Wings stemmed from a long line of professional soldiers. His grandfather had commanded the tiny band of British adventurers who had enabled Sir James Brooke to enthrone himself as the "White Rajah of Borneo." His father had succeeded him as the rajah's chief of staff, and Wings had been born in that Far Eastern outpost of the British raj.

But Wings's diplomatic skills in dealing with the enemy might have been of little avail in any other prison camp. The background and character of the *Kommandant* was a determining factor in the way we were treated, and we can only surmise that the appointment of von Lindeiner to Stalag Luft 3 reflected *Reichsmarschall* Göring's pledge that all captured Allied aircrew would be treated correctly.

Among the evidence introduced at the War Crimes Trials following the war was an assessment of Baron von Lindeiner-Wildau from the files of British Military Intelligence. It included a transcript of the interrogation of a German soldier captured sometime in 1943. Before going to the front lines, this soldier had done guard duty at Stalag Luft 3. Intelligence had questioned him about conditions at the prison camp at Sagan.

Oberst von Lindeiner, the soldier had said, "is pro-English." He said that the *Kommandant* had told the prison staff that the prisoners were not "barbaric Russians." They were Englishmen, which he said was a different proposition entirely. Further, the witness said, the *Kommandant* had actually punished guards who had shown disrespect to the prisoners.

Wings Day, of course, had very early become aware of the *Kommandant*'s attitude, although he had been somewhat disconcerted to discover a little later, when aircrew from the U.S. Army Air Corps began arriving in large numbers, that Baron von Lindeiner held the same view of Americans as he did of the Russians. In his book they were all "barbarians."

The *Kommandant*'s choice of his *Lagerfeld-webel*, his chief security officer, was in turn a reflection of his own inclinations. He was Hermann Glemnitz, who was to become a landmark in the memory of every prisoner who passed through Stalag Luft 3. Glemnitz was the chief guard, the boss, the man who kept order, who sniffed out escape attempts, who decided who should be lugged off to the cooler and for what.

Glemnitz was an ideal figure for the job. He was every inch the "tough guy," with the voice, features and bearing that would have done justice to a Hollywood version of the typical Nazi concentration camp sadist. He was in reality a first-class gentleman. At times, when some unruliness called for it, Glemnitz would pull out his pistol and wave it about with drill-sergeant bellowing; then just as quickly he would slip it back into its holster with a mischievous grin and the unspoken query: "Well, boys, how's that for acting?"

Glemnitz spoke excellent English. He had worked for many years abroad, first in England and later in railway construction in Mexico and the southwestern United States. He had a wife and three children living in Berlin. In camp he moved freely among the prisoners, frequently sitting down to share a mug of coffee or a cigarette. His sharp eye was always on the alert for signs of subversive activity, but his engaging personality and sense of humour soon forged an indefinable bond between guard and captives. He was at least twenty years senior to the average prisoner, a fact that may have lent him the aura of a father figure.

Wings Day had first made the acquaintance of Hermann Glemnitz at his first place of incarceration, the all-ranks prison camp at Barth on the Baltic coast. A bond of mutual respect had linked the pair from that time forward. Wings later recalled that it was Glemnitz's sense of humour that first attracted him to the man.

He recalled one episode at Barth, during the winter of 1941–42, when an enterprising prisoner essayed an escape disguised as, of all things, one of the *Kommandantur*'s Alsatian guard dogs.

The prisoner had equipped himself with the

sheepskin lining of an old greatcoat to simulate fur and dyed it to match the Alsatians' colour.

"And he had spent hours and days mashing up old newspapers to fashion a papier-mâché imitation of the dog's head and shoulders," said Wings. "After that, it was just a matter of waiting for a dirty, snowy night, when he planned to trot along on all fours behind one of the German guard patrols leaving the camp."

A genuine blizzard provided the ideal opportunity for the break, and everything went well until the ersatz dog had made his way through the gate into the *Kommandantur*, at which point he attracted the unwelcome attention of a real guard dog.

Glemnitz had thought it a great joke, and Wings Day never ceased to chuckle at the way Hermann had broken the news to him.

"He said we didn't need to worry; their dog hadn't harmed our dog at all. Their dog, he said, simply wanted to make love!"

One uncomfortable incident in the spring of 1943 confirmed our measure of Glemnitz. A small group of prisoners who comprised one of the many distilling-and-drinking syndicates had spent the day enjoying their monthly bash. By lockup time, when prisoners were confined to their barracks and the blackout shutters closed, one lone prisoner was still on the loose, riding high in spirit on a bellyful of triple-distilled hooch.

A guard in a watchtower yelled at him to get back to his barrack, and the prisoner responded with an obscenity. The guard levelled his rifle and fired a shot over the prisoner's head. The drunk shouted another obscenity and then took refuge inside one of the many concrete garbage incinerators spread around the compound.

There was another shot, and a chip of concrete flew from the incinerator.

The prisoner poked his head up and yelled a derisive taunt at the guard tower.

"Yah, yah, Tunisia! Yah, yah, yah!"

Another bullet spattered against the incinerator. The head disappeared momentarily and then popped up like a jack-in-the-box. Those of us watching from the barracks windows found it a fascinating performance.

"Yah, yah, Stalingrad!"

It was an infuriating taunt, and it brought a second guard tower into action. Hundreds of us watched in suspense. Every few seconds the drunk would poke his head up and yell some taunting obscenity at the towers; then duck as bullets ricochetted off his little concrete fortress. It appeared that it would be only a matter of minutes before some miscalculation would see the drunk's head blown away.

Then Hermann Glemnitz came on the scene. He came striding through the main gate, screaming at the guard towers.

"*Nicht schiessen!* Stop firing!"

There was silence.

Without a word, Glemnitz reached into the incinerator with one arm, grabbed the prisoner by the scruff of his neck, dragged him out of the box and hauled him off through the main gate, leaving him to sober up in the cooler for fifteen days.

There was another facet to Glemnitz; you sometimes had the impression that he wished to bolster prisoner morale. "Stop complaining, you fellows! If you don't like it here, you can always escape, or try to. But look at me. It's my camp and my wire; where the hell can I escape to?"

By war's end, every one of us knew Hermann Glemnitz for what he was: a loyal German soldier, an incorruptible guard and a man of good humour, maturity and judgement. At war's end it was his turn to become a prisoner, but not for long. He was shortly to be employed by the Royal Air Force as a foreman at the RAF base at Berlin's Gatow Airport. Many years later, in 1970, at a reunion of air force prisoners of war in Toronto, Hermann Glemnitz was guest of honour. As he so well deserved, Hermann was enjoying life, drawing pensions from both the Luftwaffe and the Royal Air Force.

One of the first ex-POWs to be recognized by Glemnitz when he arrived in Toronto for the 1970 reunion was Air Commodore C.D. "Red" Noble, OBE, of the Royal Canadian Air Force, who was one of a tight little knot of one-time fly-boys at the welcoming reception at the Royal York Hotel.

"I don't remember the names," said Glemnitz, "but I remember all the faces." Then, looking hard at Noble, he added, "And you are the son of a bitch who stole my flashlight!"

It had been twenty-eight years earlier. Glemnitz had been conducting a search of one of the barracks with a squad of security men. To get a closer look at some suspected item, Glemnitz had momentarily laid his big shiny flashlight on one of the bunks. In a flash it was gone. He knew at once who had taken it — the big, innocent, blue-eyed, red-headed kid who had been standing next to him all through the search. But the flashlight — the corpus delicti — had vanished. Noble had slipped it quickly to other hands, and it had joined the rest of the camp's arsenal of subversion.

By war's end, Red Noble, one of the most dedicated of the escapers, had earned a fair reputation for shoplifting. One of his most notable acquisitions was a 200-metre drum of electric lighting cable, material of great strategic importance needed by Wally Floody for the illumination of the Great Escape tunnel.

That particular exploit of Noble's cannot be better told than it was in the official transcript of evidence given at the subsequent courtmartial of *Obergefreiter* Lubos, an electrician employed by the *Kommandantur* at Stalag Luft 3. The document was among captured Luftwaffe papers presented during the postwar inquiry into the murder of the fifty officers shot by the Gestapo following the Great Escape.

Lubos, the transcript says, "brought three 200-metre drums of cable into the camp. The prisoners crowded around him." (That was a typical Noble shoplifting ploy, making a diversion of confusion.)

"One of them offered him some cigarettes, which he accepted, and asked for some of the cable, promising more cigarettes. The accused refused this offer, but left a drum of cable lying by a telegraph pole while he went about his work. When the accused left the camp he found that the third drum, which he had not needed, had disappeared. Later the cable was found in the escape tunnel, used as lighting cable."

Lubos wound up in military prison, while Red Noble, for that and other bits of studied larceny, eventually earned himself the OBE.

Another face instantly recognized by Glemnitz at that reception was that of Flight Lieutenant C. W. "Wally" Floody, OBE, of Toronto, who must rank as the outstanding Canadian POW of World War II. Floody, who had been a hardrock miner in northern Ontario before enlisting in the RCAF, was chief engineer for the multitude of tunnels at Stalag Luft 3. He is remembered primarily for the magnificent engineering involved in the Great Escape tunnel of March 1944. That tunnel, 25 feet below the surface, and equipped with electric lights, air pumping system and a tracked railroad, ran for a distance of 325 feet until it reached forest cover beyond the perimeter wire.

Glemnitz remembered Floody well. Over the nine months during which the big tunnel was under way, the Germans had known that a major operation was going on. There were, in fact, three tunnels being built simultaneously, code-named Tom, Dick and Harry. From a hundred bits of evidence and some clever deduction, Glemnitz and his men had even identified the prisoners they believed to be the "executives" involved. On one occasion, on a surprise visit to the compound, Glemnitz had noticed telltale flecks of sand on Floody's clothes.

At the Toronto confrontation, the sight of Wally

Floody triggered a sharp memory. "You still digging tunnels?" Glemnitz asked.

Floody had been one of the lucky ones involved in the Great Escape caper. In the first place, he was lucky to have survived a cave-in, being unconscious and close to death when fellow diggers dragged him to the surface. In the second instance, he had been slated to go out with the eighty-three who did manage to get through the tunnel to "freedom." He would almost certainly have been among the fifty who, when recaptured, were grabbed by the Gestapo and shot in cold blood.

He very likely owes his life to Hermann Glemnitz, for, as it turned out, Glemnitz had compiled a list of those he suspected of being involved in the tunnelling operations. A few weeks before the big tunnel was due to be finished and used, Floody and a few score other Old Kriegies and known escapers were loaded into trucks and transported to a new "escape-proof" compound a few miles distant at Fort Belaria.

Floody made another notable contribution to prison camp morale. His engineering skills extended to confectionery. By carefully husbanding some of the more choice items in the Red Cross food parcels, he had contrived to create an exciting variety of English trifle, which the camp came to know as Floody's Folly or Nightmare for Five. In later years, when Floody came to be invested by the king with the Order of the British Empire, his fellow prisoners could never quite determine whether it was in honour of his tunnels or his trifle.

VII

The Pubic Hair Contest and Other Pranks

There were several people in Stalag Luft 3 who really didn't belong there. One of them was the Dodger, as we came to call him. For the great mass of prisoners, most of whom were in their early twenties, if not in their late teens, the Dodger was a venerable figure. He was probably fifty years of age, and his white hair and dignified bearing were in sharp contrast to the appearance of the average young Kriegie. What was more, he was not a fly-boy. He didn't belong to anybody's air force, and he hadn't been shot down.

He was Major John Bigelow Dodge, DSO, DSC, MC, and he was a nephew of Winston Churchill's. Although he had been born in the United States and was the director of a New York bank in addition to other business activities, Dodge had made England his home since 1914. On the outbreak of World War II, he had enlisted in the Fifty-first Highland Division. He had been taken prisoner when the Germans overran France in 1940 and the division had been surrounded at St. Valery on the Channel coast.

The Germans planned to move some of their British Army prisoners to Germany by sea. Dodge found himself a passenger on a barge, and when it reached the River Scheldt in Holland he promptly jumped overboard. Sadly, he made contact with the wrong Hollander on reaching shore and was promptly handed over to the nearest German, who happened to be a Luftwaffe man. Included with the week's bag of Luftwaffe prisoners, he shortly found himself at the Luftwaffe interrogation centre at Oberursel near Frankfurt am Main.

The Luftwaffe wasn't particularly interested in an army major, but their chief intelligence officer, Major Theo Rumpel, who was something of an anglophile in company with many other Luftwaffe officers, treated the newcomer with special respect. His relationship with the British prime minister was one factor; another was the intervention of certain German associates of the New York bank of which Dodge was a director.

Wings Day was by that time already a prisoner

but was still being held at the interrogation centre at Oberursel. He had known Dodge in peacetime, and they had shared membership in the same London club. Rumpel had quickly noted the bond between them, and it was he who had suggested that perhaps they might like to share the remainder of their captivity.

"After all," he had said to Wings, "you and Dodge belong to the same club, so he might just as well go along with you to the RAF camp."

For the benefit of the bureaucrats in the records office in Berlin, Rumpel had conveniently made a note in Dodge's official dossier: "Seconded to the Royal Air Force."

At Stalag Luft 3 in Sagan, the Dodger had become something of a mystery man. He was a quiet, modest sort of fellow who spent most of his time reading from what we jokingly called the Lower Silesian branch of the Bodleian Library. He didn't appear to take much interest in the everyday activities of the prisoners.

He talked little about his background, but Wally Floody, who in his capacity as chief tunnel engineer spent much of his time in the company of Wings Day, who in turn shared a room with Major Dodge, came to learn something of a remarkably exciting career.

Dodge had enlisted in the Royal Naval Division on the outbreak of World War I, and earned his first decoration at Gallipoli in 1915. He ended that war as lieutenant-colonel of the Royal Sussex Regiment on the western front, with further honours, and in the years between the wars had punctuated his business career with some mysterious intelligence missions that had taken him to Burma, China and the Soviet Union. Arrested by the Soviet secret police as a spy, he had managed to escape from Russia in 1920.

The Dodger also escaped from Stalag Luft 3.

He was among the eighty-three officers who went out through Wally Floody's tunnel in the Great Escape of March 1944. He was accompanied by a young Canadian, Flight Lieutenant Jimmy Wernham, but the two men were picked up several days later while attempting to buy railway tickets at a station not far from Sagan. Wernham was shot by the Gestapo on orders from Berlin, but Major Dodge was taken to Sachsenhausen concentration camp, where he found himself reunited with Wings Day.

He was not in Sachsenhausen long. He was hustled out of his cell one morning and driven to the German Foreign Office in the Wilhelmstrasse. There followed several hours of discussion with some senior government officers. Then he was whipped away to be shirted and suited by a fashionable Berlin tailor, given suitable travel documents and some money, and sent on his way to Switzerland. He had been asked to carry some peace proposals to his uncle, Winston Churchill.

But the German diplomats were too late. By the time the Dodger had reached London and was dining with his uncle in Downing Street, Adolf Hitler had committed suicide and Germany's armed forces had surrendered.

The Dodger, however, had succeeded in getting home ahead of the rest of us.

Another irregular in the camp, like Major Dodge, was a Canadian, Philippe Gaudreault. He ought not to have been in the camp at all. He had never worn a uniform in his life and belonged to no kind of military body. He was a Québecois and an oblate priest. He had been born and brought up in Rimouski, educated at St. Paul University and the Oblate Seminary in Ottawa, and then sent, in the company of nine other oblate priests, to serve in the mission field of Basutoland in South Africa.

But he never arrived in Africa.

The ship on which the priests were travelling, the Egyptian flag liner *ZamZam*, was intercepted and sunk in the South Atlantic by the German surface raider *Atlantis*. All of the passengers and the crew, including the missionaries, were taken aboard *Atlantis* and eventually arrived in Germany.

Under the Geneva Convention, clergymen were classed as noncombatants, eligible to be repatriated to their own country. But since it would take some time to negotiate arrangements for their return home, the German authorities suggested that the ten oblate priests should be temporarily assigned as chaplains to serve in various prison camps scattered around Germany. This was how Father Gaudreault landed in Stalag Luft 3.

Shortly afterwards, several British Army chaplains, captured by the Germans in North Africa, arrived in camp. They were not prisoners long. One morning the *Kommandant* came into the camp, rounded up all the clergymen and told them to pack their bags. A Swedish ship was to take them home to Britain. They promptly packed their bags and left — all of them, that is, except Father Gaudreault.

"I have no instructions from the superior of my order," he told the *Kommandant*. "I must obey my own conscience. I shall remain here to serve my fellow prisoners."

This slightly built, dark-eyed priest, the only man behind our barbed wire who had never worn a uniform and never dropped a bomb or fired a shot, came to make a remarkable contribution to life in the camp. Morale and esprit de corps in Stalag Luft 3 were always high, and Father Gaudreault played a significant part in keeping it that way. His relationship with the prisoners was mostly one of easy, informal comradeship. He never preached. He spent most of his time sitting in on bull sessions, swapping stories, chatting about the news and answering the not infrequent questions about religion and philosophy. He enjoyed no special privileges, shared our privations and tramped alongside us through the bitter cold and the deep snows of the so-called Death March in the last days of the war.

He was intellectually honest, declining to encourage conversion to his faith. Many prisoners had sought such encouragement, but he would remind them gently that the prison camp environment was an abnormal and artificial one, not always conducive to a man's best judgement. He welcomed questions about his faith and answered them fully, but he invariably cautioned a prospective proselyte to postpone his decision until safely home again.

Father Gaudreault had had his chance to return home, along with the other chaplains, in 1942. He chose instead to stay for the remaining three years of the war as a volunteer prisoner in Stalag Luft 3, earning the admiration and respect of us all.

Another Québecois in the camp, this one in the uniform of the Royal Canadian Air Force, was Armand Rondeau, whom we came to cherish for the virtually unending, and always unintentional, entertainment he provided. Much of it derived from his hilarious coming to terms with the German language and his predilection for inventing the most preposterous German compound nouns.

Armand had been a tail gunner in the turret of a Lancaster bomber. He first won our attention when he was overheard describing himself to one of the German guards as a *Kanonhausführer*. In German parlance a *Führer* is either a pilot or a leader, or else just a driver or an operator. Armand had simply tucked this word onto what he felt was an apt description of a gun turret: a *Kanonhaus*.

Not long afterwards, it was Rondeau who dreamed up our formal name for the German who drove the big tank truck that conveyed the contents of our latrines to the farm fields on the outside.

Since the German word corresponding to the vulgar English four-letter word for excrement is *Scheiss*, Rondeau determined that the truck driver might quite properly be called a *Scheisswagen-*

führer. Then, to further distinguish him by virtue of his specific prison camp duties, he expanded this to *Kriegsgefangenenlager-scheisswagenführer* — a "prisoner-of-war-camp-shit-wagon-driver."

It was in such a manner that first Rondeau, and later the rest of the camp, would formally greet the truck driver on his daily rounds: *"Guten Morgen, Herr Kriegsgefangenenlager-scheisswagenführer!"*

At first the driver was understandably insulted, but since the greeting was usually accompanied by a Red Cross cigarette or two, he soon came to accept his title with a wryly good-natured smile.

The entertainment contribution of Armand Rondeau inevitably sparks vivid memories of another superlative entertainer, an RAF flight lieutenant by the name of Foo McHardy. I never did know his real name; everyone called him Foo, but nobody knew why. Foo was Welsh, a tall, gangling, fair-haired blond with a wispy, reddish moustache. He had been educated at the best British public schools and on graduation had joined the RAF to become a pilot. He was shot down over Germany.

In many secondary schools it is a tradition for graduating classes, in their yearbooks, to nominate one member of their class as the student most likely to succeed. Had Stalag Luft 3 been an educational institution, which perhaps in many ways it was, we should almost unanimously have chosen Foo McHardy as the man most likely to make a great name for himself in the years to come.

Foo was a persuasive public speaker with leadership qualities and a lively, fertile imagination. We prophesied an academic career of world-shaking impact for him and harboured the belief that before long he would be sharing space with Albert Einstein in the Institute for Advanced Learning at Princeton University. Failing that, he might become prime minister of Britain, or at the very least president of the Chase Manhattan Bank.

Foo made notable contributions to prison camp morale. There was, for instance, his conviction that prisoners ought not to recognize German time, which was Central European Time; yet he ruled out British double daylight saving time as impractical. He introduced instead what came to be known as McHardy Time, which rated the hours as plus or minus the twice-daily German roll call, or *Appell.* Noon lunch, for instance, coming four hours after the eight o'clock morning Appell, was deemed by the McHardy mess as served at four o'clock!

He also initiated the tradition of the Duchy, a fascinating order of nobility in which the members, on a weekly roster system, would designate one of their number the Duke, who was eligible for a broad range of perks and privileges. The Duke would have his breakfast brought to him in his bunk, was carried to and from *Appell* on the back of another prisoner and at all times carried around his neck a splendid medallion proclaiming him to be the Duke. It was a popular and typical McHardy innovation.

Foo was an advanced mathematician and to this day is still remembered by many old prisoners for the lecture he delivered, before almost the entire camp, on the life and works of the renowned

French mathematician Henri Marchant. None of us, of course, had ever heard of Marchant, but McHardy made it abundantly clear that we all ought to have heard of him. Marchant's revolutionary system of numeration was so new that McHardy had been the first man in camp to hear of it. He had had much correspondence, he said by way of introduction, with fellow mathematicians at Cambridge. It was a masterful lecture.

Foo prefaced his remarks with an intimate review of Marchant's boyhood and early schooling, touched on some early trials in family life and spoke with sympathy of Marchant's only and rather tragic romance. Describing much of his later work, Foo dealt in detail with Marchant's difficulties with the French Academy. He then went on to explain the Marchant System, going to great lengths to demonstrate its superiority to both our conventional numeration and the binary system.

Most of us didn't even pretend to understand it but went away in a state of breathless awe, saying, "What a magnificent brain that man has!" But for those whose education had encompassed the mysteries of higher calculus, McHardy's unveiling of the Marchant System touched off a week of furious controversy. The camp's few real savants were divided into two schools; they were either pro-Marchant or anti-Marchant.

Neither camp ever quite forgave Foo when he casually let it be known, about a week later, that both Henri Marchant and his system were merely figments of the McHardy imagination. As for the rest of us, the uneducated, we were more than ever convinced that McHardy's platform magic couldn't fail to conquer the world.

Many years after the war, while on a visit to England, I ran across one of Foo's Welsh compatriots, Gwyn Martin, who had shared the Stalag Luft 3 years with McHardy and me. I asked him about Foo McHardy, and Gwyn smiled wistfully.

"Foo? He's doing just fine."

"University president?" I suggested.

Gwyn laughed. "Better than that! He paints tavern signs. Public-house signs, you know. Bull and Blanket, Pig and Whistle, Elephant and Castle. Foo has a fine hand for that sort of thing. Nice eye for colour, too. Loves lots of brilliance. He was through our town a week or two ago, did a bang-up job at the Maid of Mercy. Put a bloody big golden halo on her."

I was stunned. "But can he make any kind of living at that sort of thing?"

Gwyn had that wistful look again. "What more does he want? He takes his time painting the sign; then takes his pay in bed and board. Stays at the inn, eats all he wants and drinks even more, spends the evenings playing darts and chess with the locals; then when his credit is all used up he moves on, looking for the next sign to paint. Been at it twenty years or more now. I guess Foo has seen every village in England and had a drink at every pub. Can you tell me of a better life than that?"

Those of us in Stalag Luft 3 who rated Foo McHardy the prisoner most likely to succeed just may have judged him better than we knew.

It was McHardy, too, who promoted the celebrated pubic-hair contest in the summer of 1943. One morning a notice about the contest was found posted to the wall of the camp latrine, the accepted notice board for the listing of public events. The notice read as follows:

*   *   *

WHITE PUBIC HAIR

A grand prize of one entire
Canadian Red Cross food parcel
is offered as a prize to the first
prisoner able to produce a white
pubic hair. The hair must be seen
in situ, and verified by the
Judging Committee. The contest will
end on the 30th of the month.

*   *   *

An additional Red Cross food parcel, especially the preferred Canadian one, would be welcome in anybody's mess, and we felt sure that Flight Lieutenant George Harsh, a member of the same eight-man mess as Wally Floody and me, would be a sure winner.

Harsh, an American from Atlanta, who looked every inch a Southern gentleman, was reputed to be the oldest man in the camp. He didn't tell anyone how old he was, but he had snow-white hair and a splendid white moustache, and when he was feeling low he would huddle in his bunk and tell us that "in the next war I'm going to tell them my right age!"

But all George's white hairs, as it turned out on careful inspection, were exclusively above his belt. To everyone's amazement, the winner, and indeed the one and only entrant in the contest, was a black-haired stripling of a fighter pilot little more than twenty years of age.

George Harsh is a story in himself.

In a camp where the overwhelming majority of men were in their late teens or early twenties, white-haired men were few. There were some whose hair had turned white from the anxiety and tensions of harrowing combat experience. But George Harsh was different; he had come white-haired to the Royal Canadian Air Force when he enlisted in Toronto in 1940. An American citizen, he had just been paroled from a life sentence for murder, after spending twelve terrible years on the notorious Georgia chain gang.

George had come to Canada hoping to make a new start by enlisting in one of Canada's services. Somebody told him about the air force. Another ex-con he had bumped into tipped him off about how to handle the troublesome problem of his criminal record:

"When you get to that part in the application felony, all you do is write down 'no'!"

So George had written "no" to the query and, not long after, with several months of training behind him, found himself a commissioned officer and an air gunner in the Royal Canadian Air Force — and on his way overseas.

George Harsh died in 1980 in the Sunnybrook Veterans' Hospital in Toronto. I remember him as one of the finest men it has ever been my good fortune to have as a friend. In prison camp he was an outstanding personality. There was a certain warmth about him and a maturity that earned the respect and admiration of younger men. His intellectual stature was manifest, and few officers in the camp were so well informed about as many things as George Harsh. He had an entertaining wit and, apart from occasional brief spells of depression, a great good humour.

Few people in Stalag Luft 3 knew about George's criminal background. While a senior at Oglethorpe University in Georgia, George and another student, in search of adventure, had engaged in a string of armed holdups. The adventure had ended in a supermarket shoot-out in which George's Colt .45 automatic had snuffed out the lives of two store clerks. He had been found guilty and sentenced to die in the electric chair, but through a complicated technicality the sentence had been commuted to life on the Georgia chain gang.

One of the very few who knew George's story was Wally Floody. When Wally was commissioned by the Escape Committee to build Harry, the ambitious tunnel of The Great Escape, he had recommended that George Harsh take on the job of security officer, to protect the tunnelling operation from the German security force.

As Wally put it to him after the appointment had been ratified: "George, I'll bet this is the only time you'll ever get a job because you're an ex-con!"

George had at first protested that he didn't want the job, but Floody had been adamant. "We need a man on this job who has had experience. How many men are there in this camp who have had twelve years in prison?"

George took the job. Nine months later the tunnel spewed out eighty-three prisoners in one of the most celebrated mass escapes in recent times. George Harsh's security system had been without a flaw.

VIII

Jane, Fanny and Company

Wow! Hear the latest, old boy? Twenty-five nurses have just been taken prisoner. They're on their way here now!"

It was just one more "latrine rumour," the kind of phony news dreamed up in the camp washhouse.

"Yeah, twenty-five of them, they say, and right from the States. Shot down in North Africa, in a Yank Dakota. Boy, things are looking up!"

There was not, of course, one grain of truth in

119

it, something most of us knew the moment we heard it. In RAF vernacular, it was not "pukka gen." But it was the kind of latrine rumour we loved to hear, very definitely the stuff of which prison camp morale was made.

There were no women in German camps for Allied POWs (unlike those that held Russia's female front-line fighters), but by some mysterious sorcery, a woman's spell drifted through the barbed wire to become a vital component of the prisoner-of-war psyche. In one metaphysical form or another, the other sex was always close to us.

News about women rated on a par with news about the war, which came to us mostly through our underground radio link, plus the daily communiqué over the German public-address system. News about women came from many sources, including the new prisoners fresh from home. The Germans thrust them at us every few weeks in groups we came to call the purges.

The purges were mobbed the moment the gates closed behind them. Already disoriented and confused, they were invariably mystified by their reception. They appeared to find some difficulty in understanding why the thing uppermost in the minds of old prisoners was "What happened to Jane?"

Jane, as so many veterans fondly recall, was the heroine of a popular British newspaper comic strip. Jane was marvellously endowed with tantalizing legs that dissolved upwards into almost unbearable callipygian beauty. Jane's story was one exciting and hilarious story after another, all marked by the common denominator that Jane was regularly stripped of most, if not all, of her clothing.

The newcomers were taken aback.

"Jane? Jane? Oh, yes . . . hey, Bill, what was the last episode of Jane? Oh, yeah, she was trapped by some Nazi spies but she managed to escape. Jumped out a window, and her dress got snagged in some brambles and she got stripped right down to her bra. Oh, sure, Jane's doing just fine!"

The adventures of Jane were but one of the many influences keeping alive the libido of thousands of POWs over the long years of captivity. But whereas Jane was the creation of a cartoonist (who ought to have had a World War II decoration), a myriad of other Janes lived in the flesh and in the imaginations of all those men without women.

There were, for instance, the Hollywood film stars, whose eight-by-ten glossies, courtesy of mail from home, brightened the dingy recesses of the three-tier bunks. There were Betty Grable and Lana Turner, Rita Hayworth and Veronica Lake, and a score of other lovelies. Then there were the more personal pinups of the girls the boys had left behind — the hometown sweethearts, mostly.

I remember well the pinup of a Halifax girl, a ravishing member of the Junior League set who had kindled a torch in the hearts of a never-ending succession of servicemen passing through that East Coast Canadian port on their way overseas. Her picture, sultry and inviting, was pinned to the wall next to the bunk of an RCAF navigator who had courted her furiously during his three weeks' embarkation leave at Y Depot in Halifax.

That particular pinup provoked one of the rare cases of violence in our camp. A new prisoner, with a much more recent Halifax romance fresh in his memory, was stunned to confront his inamorata staring at him from the shelter of another man's bunk. There were words, then blows, a split lip and a bloody nose. In a matter of days the pinup discreetly disappeared.

Affairs of the heart were a welcome source of prison camp gossip and entertainment. Some were more sensational than others. Few could rival that told by a Czech fighter pilot who arrived with the almost incredible story that he had been deliberately shot down not by a German but by his own flight commander.

The Czech had been flying the number two position covering his flight commander in a dogfight with Germans over the north coast of France. Quite suddenly, in the middle of the melee, he said, his flight commander had throttled back his Spitfire, positioned it above and behind him and opened fire on him. The Czech had baled out of his burning Spit and had been lucky to survive.

He was a big, dark handsome fellow.

"When I get back to England I'm going to kill that bastard," he raged. His explanation for it was quite straightforward.

"He was jealous, that's all. But just because I was taking his wife out was no reason to want to kill me, was it?"

The Czech was cheated of his threatened revenge. Within a few weeks we had word that his flight commander, in the RAF vernacular, had "gone for a Burton."

Then there was *Vorlager* Fanny.

We attached that alliterative handle to the rather pretty young German woman who worked as a secretary in the *Vorlager*, the block of administrative offices just the other side of the wire near the main gate.

It had started innocently enough with Fanny occasionally coming to the office window, primping coyly and giving us a flirtatious wave of the hand. We gave her all the encouragement we could, and Fanny became less inhibited. She enlisted the aid of some of the Luftwaffe admin officers and began to stage an elaborate and provocative tableau at the office window. One of the officers would grab her around the waist with one arm, kiss her in an ecstatically tight embrace, bend her back over a desk and then with his free arm slowly pull down the window shade.

We applauded wildly and over the years were rewarded with many encores. *Vorlager* Fanny is a fond and happy memory.

For those who could read German, the daily newspapers afforded yet another kind of surrogate romance. The personal columns of German dailies sometimes ran to whole pages in a single issue. In a land where virtually every able-bodied male was at the front, or had already met the *Heldentod*, each day brought its plaintive quota of little notices, inserted by hopeful females looking for a man.

A long winter's evening would often find a huddle of three or four prisoners thumbing avidly through the heartthrob columns of the *Völkischer Beobachter* and the *Frankfurter Zeitung*.

"Here's just the one for you, Jim. Geli, it says, age twenty, blonde and slender, likes theatre and walks in the woods, prefers an older man. Say, that's you, Jim — you're twenty-eight!"

"And, oh boy, listen to this! Her name's Annaliese, Box 51. Warm, sympathetic nature and lonely. I'll think about that one. But will you get a load of this? Marlene, age twenty-three . . ."

Stories in the apocryphal category, such as that of the shot-down nurses, included an entire repertory involving camps where Russian women prisoners were held. One of the most popular scenarios, which made the rounds about every six months, followed an escaping Brit or Yank — always from some other unnamed camp! — who had found sanctuary by wriggling through the wire into a Russian women's camp. Three days and nights later, so the grim story went, he had surrendered to the Germans, more dead than alive, and was now recuperating in the lazaret.

Only one member of our community could be credited with any kind of romantic adventure beyond the barbed wire. He was Flight Lieutenant Joe Ricks of the RAF, a Czech who was a dedicated and an indefatigable escaper. His true name was concealed to protect his family still living in Czechoslovakia. Joe was a sturdy bundle of vitality and optimism — short, stocky and strong as an ox.

Dancing blue eyes and a mischievous grin that permanently creased his happy Slav face could make him an odds-on winner in any encounter with the opposite sex.

Before coming to Stalag Luft 3, Joe had been held at a Wehrmacht camp at Schubin, in Occupied Poland. His fluency in both German and Polish quickly helped him to make contacts outside the camp, and the guards appeared not to mind when Joe shouted greetings in Polish to some of the pretty Polish peasant girls on the other side of the wire.

Before long the over-the-wire conversations led to clandestine correspondence. Polish civilian workers frequently came into the camp on business and were persuaded to carry notes to and from the outside. One of these was the driver of the sewage cart, whose job it was to empty the camp latrines. The honey cart, as the prisoners called it, was a big cylindrical tank with a circular hatch on top, and at first sight of it Joe Ricks viewed it as an ideal vehicle for escape.

The Polish driver, who was the father of one of the girls who appeared at the wire, co-operated. On the day of the escape, the honey cart had been swilled out and Joe, armed with a bottle of eau de cologne in addition to his escape paraphernalia, crawled into the tank.

Joe didn't make it back to Britain. But he was on the loose for three months. Part of the time he had spent in the company of one of the Polish girls who had been waving to him from across the wire. He was eventually recaptured in Warsaw, guest of a

Jewish family in the ghetto, and spent several weeks in a Polish civilian concentration camp before being shipped to Stalag Luft 3.

The concentration camp was a frightful place, Joe reported.

"It was more of a madhouse than a prison. The strangest things happened. One of the barracks was set aside as a chapel; every Sunday a priest came in to say Mass. The Germans kept the men separate from the women in the chapel — they had rigged up a screen of chicken wire right down the middle. Every Mass the place was packed. It was so dark and dingy and crowded that no one paid any attention to the lovemaking going on through the chicken wire."

Joe's was a strictly vicarious contribution to our sex-starved libidos, and there were others of the same secondhand quality.

The German guards, too, sometimes unwittingly fed our frustrated sexuality. For those of us who had come to know one of the guards on a more than casual level, the acquaintance could be a channel for some vicarious sex. There is a bit of Casanova in every man, and with a little prompting a guard might boast of his philandering, thus playing a surrogate role in our famished fantasies.

There was Hans, for instance, whom I had come to know well over the years. Today Hans (not his real name) lives happily with his wife and family in West Germany. His not unforgivable wartime indiscretions shall remain forever concealed.

His wife and four children had been bombed out of their home and now dwelt in a refugee area where he saw them only seldom. But Hans had a mistress in the little town of Sagan, adjacent to the camp. Emmi also had four children, but her husband was serving with the Wehrmacht infantry on the Russian front.

Hans called Emmi's husband a bad man: *"Ein böser Mensch!"*

"Why, what's wrong with him?" I asked.

"He runs around with other women!"

Hans's affair with Emmi titillated us. After he had enjoyed a weekend leave, we never neglected on Monday morning to wheedle out of him every intimate detail of his rendezvous. One such Monday-morning report was memorable. Hans had been to visit Emmi on the Sunday afternoon.

"Ach! It was no good. Nothing went right. We sent the kids out to play and locked the door. But they kept coming back and hammering at the door and saying, *'Mutti, Mutti, was ist los?* [Mummy, what's the matter?]' "

"We had to let them in. The day was ruined."

"Hans," I said, "you should do the way we do it back in Canada." I spoke as the father of four. "On Sunday afternoons we pack the kids off to Sunday school. It's the best afternoon of the week!"

Hans grimaced and swore. "That's what's wrong with Germany," he said. "No Sunday school anymore!"

Then there was mail from home. It came predominantly from wives, sweethearts, mistresses and mothers. A prisoner's first letter was almost invariably from a woman, usually a wife or mother. During the first few days of captivity, it was something to which the prisoner looked forward with an increasingly poignant and urgent longing. The woman's touch was never needed more. Usually that first letter did not arrive for several months, and when it came it was good for days and even weeks of hungry reading.

In most cases the first letter was a sentimental surfeit of affection and sympathy. Some prisoners were quite surprised by the depth of feeling conveyed. It was so nice to know she felt like that; it made a man feel good. In my own case, the first letter from home had been rather more prosaic; the opening line was, "Thanks to Hitler, I know where you are at night!"

The feminine mail from home was not uniformly welcome. For some single prisoners, and especially after the Allies had landed in Normandy and the prospect of liberation began to loom as something more than a dream, there was a sudden apprehension lest the long years of intimate correspondence come to be interpreted as some kind of ironclad engagement to marry.

Armand Rondeau was in this situation. Armand had begun to worry about his problem even before the Invasion. He had been "in the bag" since 1941. In the possession of cigarettes, he had become one of the more affluent among us. He had not one but two devoted girlfriends living in Toronto, luckily unknown to each other, and they had been faithfully mailing him cigarette parcels at the rate of about one a month. There were a thousand cigarettes in every carton. These gifts had enabled Armand to become something of a big wheel in the camp's black market. In Kriegie parlance, he was in the rackets.

We enjoyed teasing Armand about the source of his affluence.

"You're under an obligation, Armand. You can't get out of it. Honour bound and all that, after all they've done for you. Your only problem is deciding which one it's going to be."

Armand was sweating all right.

"Geez! I hardly knew them. Only took 'em out two or three times. Met Daisy when I first got to Manning Pool down at the Exhibition Grounds. Then while I was at Bombing and Gunnery School at Jarvis I took a forty-eight in Toronto and met Betty at a dance at Sunnyside. They were both nice kids, lots of fun. But the way they've been writing me lately it seems they figure when I get home it's going to be man and wife. Geez, I don't go for that stuff!"

We were fond of Armand. He was such good company, and he had always been generous with his cigarettes. But his dilemma entertained us immensely, and we enjoyed watching him squirm when we talked about the technicalities of breach-of-promise suits.

But Armand was a sharp lad, and he found a way out. He burst in on us one evening wearing a broad grin, a mischievous glint in his eyes.

"I think I've fixed 'em good," he said.

"Who you talking about?"

"Those dames in Toronto — both of 'em. Daisy and Betty. I've just written to them. Same letter to both of 'em. See, I fixed a date way on in

September, just to be sure they get the letters in time.

"I told 'em, did they remember the way we used to sit in that corner booth in Diana Sweets and hold hands? See, that's where I always took 'em after a show, like. You know, that Diana Sweets on Bloor Street, up there by the museum. I took Daisy once to the museum, too, to see the mummies.

"Anyway, I told 'em if they went to Diana Sweets on September the twenty-fifth, at about eight o'clock, and looked around those booths at the back near the kitchen door, they'd find someone with an important message from me. Something they'd want to hear. I made it sound mysterious, like. What d'ya think of that, eh?"

We were impressed.

And so, too, as we later surmised, were Daisy and Betty. After September there were no more letters, and the cigarettes stopped coming. That didn't matter much, really, because by that time it looked as if liberation was right around the corner. In any event, our stock of Red Cross and other cigarettes had never been higher.

As for Armand, the sudden termination of his embarrassing correspondence brought a triumphant kind of release. "Brains," he would explain to us over and over again. "When you're dealing with women, you have to use your brains!"

Whenever sex is discussed in the context of prison life, there is inevitably a question asked about homosexuality. In a community of men without women, is the incidence of homosexuality likely to increase? Since there is a minimum of privacy in camp life, it was only to be expected that what deviation existed would be more than ordinarily conspicuous. There were instances of such relationships; we were aware of them, but they were few.

Most of us never gave the subject a thought, but Major Edward Monteuis, the camp medical officer, seems to have entertained a notion that new prisoners might feel some apprehension lest a prolonged separation from female company wreak havoc on their normal libido. He frequently took the occasion to reassure us.

"Don't worry about it. If you were fated to be queer, it would have happened long before you got to this place. Sure, it may be a little more obvious here, but the percentage of deviation in a prison camp is no different than it is back home. All that stuff about prisons changing your sex life is just a lot of rot. Forget it!"

Sex talk probably consumed more time among prisoners of war than among men living in a normal and "free" society. Men who had been prisoners for a year or more came to discuss the mysteries of sex, and their own personal experiences and predilections, with a frankness rarely found elsewhere. It was not a case of boasting; it was a combination of sublimation and analytical retrospection, with the torment of denial finding relief through resurrecting the delights of yesterday.

One had the feeling that when prisoners were not talking about sex they were thinking about it. I remember one prisoner, his hope of early liberation rising with the increasingly optimistic war news, who with no provocation at all suddenly almost screamed at us:

"I've just written my wife — told her to get some new, pretty wallpaper for the bedroom ceiling. After I get home, that's all she's going to be looking at for the next six months!"

I have no way of knowing who suffered most from their long enforced celibacy, the single men or the married. What is certain is that for married prisoners the prison camp years did have a positive effect on the stability of their marriages in later years. Some testimony to this effect came in late 1983 from a Stalag Luft 3 alumnus, Anthony Pengelly of Toronto.

Pengelly had been a leading figure in camp entertainment circles, and his active and imaginative personality had made an outstanding contribution to prison camp morale. He had directed sports events, played a big part in our theatre program and still had had time to work in the forgery section of the escape organization.

Back home after the war, Pengelly progressed rapidly in the business world, becoming one of Canada's top executives in corporate marketing and public relations. He also kept in close touch with his old POW comrades. In a television interview in 1983 he revealed that he had conducted a survey on the marital status of members of the RCAF Prisoners-of-War Association. The result: not a single divorce among couples who were married before the husband became a prisoner of war.

The subject had often been discussed at the Air

Force POW reunions that have taken place in Canada at five-year intervals ever since 1945. Wives attending these reunions were often asked what changes they had noticed in the husband's personality as a result of his captivity. Without exception, every woman had said emphatically that the man they got back from prison camp was a marked improvement over the original model.

One wife put it more succinctly than most: "What every husband needs is a few good years behind barbed wire!"

There were periods in prison, however, in which our interest in the opposite sex was diminished. When the Red Cross parcels failed to arrive and rations were short, thoughts of food more than matched our concupiscence.

Perhaps the most desirable of Red Cross luxury foods came in the little cans of Borden's Sweetened Condensed Milk. On the black market they commanded a price of a thousand cigarettes. Many prisoners developed a delirious addiction to the stuff. One prisoner revealed the intensity of his craving when he confided his plans for his first hours at home after liberation:

"I'm going to go out and buy a whole case of Borden's Sweetened Condensed Milk. Then I'm going to open all the cans and fill a two-gallon bucket. Then I am going to strip my wife naked, pour the stuff all over her and lick it all off!"

This tendency was never better illustrated than in the last weeks of the war when there was a competition among the camp's artists for the best cartoon illustrating a prisoner's homecoming.

The winning picture, thumbtacked to an honoured space on the latrine wall, portrayed a newly freed POW, dufflebag over his shoulder, hurrying up the garden path to greet his wife at the door of a typical English cottage. A clinging, diaphanous negligee revealed a wifely figure of such voluptuous charm as to seduce a monk.

The cartoon's caption?

"What have you got to eat, dear?"

IX

Daredevils and Capitalists

I f prison life was largely communal, it only served to make examples of individual initiative more conspicuous. Some prisoners stood out in the crowd, sometimes through exhibitions of personal courage, sometimes through the force of personality or the will to excel. Two of the most memorable examples of such initiative were the audacious and breathtaking Nichols and Toft escape in the summer of 1943 and the success of a commercial private enterprise, the only one of its kind, known as Foodacco.

Significantly, one prisoner, Flight Lieutenant Ken Toft of the Royal Air Force, was a principal in both the dramatic escape attempt and the highly successful business venture.

I was a spectator, heart in mouth, of the escape drama. Now there were many bigger escapes from Stalag Luft 3, and more celebrated ones. There was the Great Escape of March 1944, which later became the subject of "The Great Escape," one of Hollywood's finest films about World War II, and the Wooden Horse escape, also to attain a degree of immortality through book and screen. But no escape attempt could ever quite match the Nichols and Toft escapade for sheer cold courage and hair-raising, cliff-hanging suspense.

Under the eyes of the guard towers, in the naked light of a summer noonday sun, two men calmly crossed the deadly no-man's-land between the trip-wire and the high, double-wired camp fence, spent twenty minutes cutting their way through the wire and then strolled nonchalantly to freedom on the other side. It was the impossible happening before our eyes in the broad light of day.

"It's all done with mirrors," was the way Nichols jokingly explained the plan before putting it to the test. It was a technically ingenious scheme but one in which a single slip, a miscalculation of even a split second, would invite instant death from the guns in the guard towers.

The idea originated from the mind of Flight Lieutenant "Nick" Nichols, a casual, seemingly slaphappy young American who came from the Ozark mountains of Arkansas. He looked what he was — a farm boy who had given up the farm for the excitement of aviation. He had drifted west from the Ozarks to California, where he had learned to fly. Then he had made a precarious living from barnstorming and crop dusting.

In 1940 he had sold his rugged old Stearman crop duster, made his way to England and joined the Eagle Squadron of the RAF. He had been flying a Hurricane over the French coast when he was shot down and made a prisoner.

Nick shared a room with six others and me. We enjoyed his tales of the crop-dusting flyboy fraternity in the cottonfields of Dixie but somehow found it hard to credit his common sense when he first told us about his scheme for getting through the wire to freedom. It was the most harebrained escape plan we had ever heard.

He hadn't told us about the idea until he had already submitted it to the Escape Committee. Wings Day and Wing Commander Jimmy Buckley, who was at that time heading the committee, had listened with interest but hadn't been convinced.

"It's just that I can't quite make them see it the way I see it," Nick said. "I know it will work. And I'm going to show them how. I'm going to make a model for them."

He made the model.

He had purloined one of the biggest flat bake pans he could find, one of the pieces of cookhouse equipment our tinbashers had fashioned by hammering out old tin cans. This was to be his sandbox. Painstakingly, over a period of days, working with matchsticks and a spool of white thread, he constructed a fascinating scale model of the fence, complete with all the guard towers or, as we called them, the goon boxes.

The wire enclosing the camp was a formidable obstacle. Even to reach it one would first have to cover a ten-yard open stretch of sand designated as a kind of no-man's-land and cordoned off on the prisoners' side by a single strand of wire, about two feet high, known as the trip-wire or warning wire. Prisoners understood that even to place a hand on this trip-wire was to invite a shot from the guard tower. Any attempt to make a dash from the trip-wire to the fence was tantamount to suicide.

The wire itself was a double row of ten-foot-high fences, set about six feet apart, with strands of heavy barbed wire set at about six-inch intervals up the stalwart posts. Between the two fences there was a continuous dense roll of barbed wire, and the fences were straddled by the guard towers at intervals of about one hundred yards.

"But there's a blind spot," said Nick.

And his sandbox model showed plainly that there was. At a point midway between the towers, the barrier presented by the line of fenceposts presented a barrier to the line of sight from the towers. This barrier, along with the density of the rolled-up wire between the fences, would render a man invisible from the towers once he had reached the inner side of the fence and just as invisible as he made his way under the rolled wire between the fences.

"Just give us a second's diversion while we

jump over the trip-wire and make the dash to the fence and we're home free. It's a piece of cake!''

The Escape Committee looked long and hard at Nichols's sandbox model and then gave Nick the nod. They would arrange the diversion. Nick had already picked Ken Toft to accompany him. A date was set, and the break was scheduled for a midday, daylight operation. Daylight permitted the necessary organization of the diversions. Daylight also found the guards without the hair-trigger alertness that characterized the night-hour watch.

It was in so many ways unlike any other escape in the Stalag's history. For one thing, it was an escape of which every single prisoner in the camp had to know about beforehand. Normally, details of a planned escape were restricted to as few persons as possible, for obvious reasons of security. In this instance, everyone had to know. There was too great a risk that some prisoner, ignorant of what was afoot, might stop to gape at so astonishing a sight and by his behaviour alert a guard in his tower. Prisoners were told to go about their normal business in the camp and to pay no attention to whatever unusual activity they might see around the perimeter.

The diversions were programmed on a split-second schedule, each one timed by synchronized watches. At the designated zero-second, some strange things happened simultaneously in front of each one of the guard towers. A spirited fist fight, realistically including a bloodied nose, drew the attention of one of the towers. At the next tower down the line, some of the boys dribbling a football around the field kicked it offside into the wire immediately under the tower. The guard at once leaned over the rail curiously to follow its trajectory.

Nichols and Toft vaulted lightly over the tripwire and made the dash to the fence. They had not been seen.

For the next twenty minutes, from our gallery seats inside the barracks, we watched wordlessly. From inside the compound the two prone figures were visible to everyone. We could see Nick carefully plying his homemade wirecutters; then we watched as the two wriggled their way, inch by inch, under the rolled-up wire and cut their way through the lower strands of the outer fence.

Then they were clear of the wire.

We saw them rise to their feet and begin a slow, casual stroll into the woods on the other side. We were just beginning to relax when we saw the guard in one of the towers suddenly turn and look in their direction.

Once again we caught our breath.

The guard was raising his rifle, looking intently at the two figures disappearing into the trees. Then just as suddenly he lowered the rifle and turned to resume his surveillance of the camp.

"That was one smart guard," was the way Jimmy Buckley explained it later. "He was thinking fast. Once he saw the boys walking away from the wire, he twigged to what had happened. He knew they were escaping prisoners, all right. But he guessed, correctly, that they must have made it through the wire close to his tower. It was better to keep mum and remain in ignorance than to risk a court-martial. He was smart!''

Nichols and Toft were not free long. They were recaptured two days later, hiding out in a lumber-yard while waiting between trains. On their return to Sagan they were sentenced to the customary fifteen days in the cooler, the solitary confinement cell.

But on their first night in the cooler, they had some cheering consolation. They had a visit from no less than the *Kommandant*, old Baron von Lindeiner-Wildau himself, who presented them with a bottle of whisky. He admired their courage, he said.

There was an important sequel to the Nichols and Toft escape. German security personnel carefully examined the breach cut in the wire. We could see them making observations from the adjacent guard towers and could guess that they were drawing the appropriate conclusions. As a result, additional guards were enlisted to maintain a permanent, twenty-four-hour sentry patrol on the outside of every prison camp compound. This innovation applied not only to Stalag Luft 3 but to every prison camp in Germany.

At war's end, British Intelligence concluded that the Nichols-Toft escapade had come to immobilize the equivalent of an entire division of German troops for the remainder of the war.

The spirit that sent Ken Toft on his audacious thrust through the wire may also have had something to do with his involvement in the creation of

Foodacco, the trading organization that became a vital part of camp organization at Stalag Luft 3. His partner was an energetic and ambitious young Canadian, Flight Lieutenant Ted Kipp of Winnipeg. The pair had previously been incarcerated in a camp at Warburg, and it was there on the Baltic coast that they had originally launched their business enterprise. They brought it with them when they were transferred to Stalag Luft 3.

Foodacco was an agency of great convenience. Many prisoners who enjoyed regular receipts of cigarettes from friends and next of kin found Foodacco an emporium where they could purchase a wide range of goods with their surplus cigarettes. For prisoners and guards alike, cigarettes had become the standard unit of exchange. A prisoner with more cigarettes than he needed could brighten his life considerably, and many prisoners who didn't smoke used their fags to keep themselves in comparative luxury.

A Hershey chocolate bar, out of the regular Red Cross food parcels, could be purchased at Foodacco for two hundred cigarettes. A much more delectable item, a can of Borden's Sweetened Condensed Milk, sold for a thousand. Cigarettes, apart from the single packs usually included in the Red Cross parcels, arrived in cartons of a thousand, and many prisoners might at any one time have a hoard of two, three or more cartons.

Kipp and Toft, the proprietors of Foodacco, purchased their wares from prisoners at a price slightly below that at which they sold them. They might make a profit of ten or twenty cigarettes on the sale of a can of condensed milk.

Most of us looked upon Foodacco as a useful and appreciated service. None but a negligible minority had any complaint about Kipp and Toft's doing business for a profit. Many prisoners had occupied themselves in various ways to earn the few cigarettes that would make the difference between "penury" and a reasonable "standard of living." I had myself, in the first few months of captivity, engaged in a laundry business. A pair of socks brought five cigarettes; a shirt, ten. I was doing quite well until a line full of clients' wash blew away in a gale and my business reputation went with it.

There were some complaints, however, and in the summer of 1943 Wing Commander Day, on behalf of the senior British officer, addressed the problem. There must be a referendum, he said; the prisoners would vote whether Foodacco should be retained as a private enterprise institution run by Kipp and Toft or whether the agency should become a community nonprofit foundation.

It was a spirited campaign on both sides, heavy with all the overtones of the classic "free enterprise versus socialism" debate. There were soapbox speeches, a plethora of rhetoric and scathing editorials pinned to the latrine wall. Informal pre-election polls pointed to a clear-cut victory for Kipp and Toft private enterprise, and the vote itself confirmed this.

But Wing Commander Day had the final word.

Ignoring the vote, and by virtue of the over-riding authority of the senior Allied officer, he decreed that in the best interests of the camp Foodacco must be operated as a co-operative community enterprise. The ensuing profits, he said, would be turned over to the camp kitchen and, more significantly, to the Escape Committee. It was, he said, a matter of "a war economy."

Many prisoners professed to find some irony in Wings Day's decision. After all, it was well known to everyone that Wings was an old-school-tie English aristocrat and a true-blue Tory to boot. His preference for a "socialistic" Foodacco was seen as uncharacteristic and in some vague way traitorous. Some less charitable critics attributed his aberration to "barbed wire psychosis." Like some other Old Kriegies, they hinted, he was around the bend.

X

Namentausch

Joe Ricks's grin was wider than ever the morning he told me it was time to think of escaping again. But it was not the prospect of another romantic dash for freedom that sparked his good humour. He had just come from a visit to Group Captain Massey, our senior Allied officer, and Joe was much amused. Massey had wanted a report on some security matter and Joe, along with several senior officers, had been summoned to a nine o'clock meeting in the group captain's cubicle.

"We knocked on the door and he told us to come in," Joe said. "Then he said would we mind waiting a few minutes? He was sitting with his bad leg resting on a stool. And Mackenzie was there, sitting on another stool with a book in his hands. Mackenzie had been reading to him." Mackenzie was a young Canadian who had lost his leg in a crash, and both he and Massey were due for repatriation as wounded to England.

"So we just stood there, and Groupie turned and looked at Mackenzie like he was waiting for him to start reading again. It was funny. Mackenzie looked at us, and then back at Groupie, and his face got as red as a beet.

"'Go on, Mackenzie,' Groupie said, and Mackenzie sort of coughed and looked like he was going to die. And then Groupie told him again, like he was a little annoyed, so Mackenzie picked up the book and began to read.

"'. . . and the little elf went jumping from stump to stump,' he read. The little elf went jumping from stump to stump — it was some fairy tale. Can you beat it? The little elf . . . My God, Brownie, it's time we got to hell out of here. What do you say?"

Joe had an idea, he said.

"Maybe we'll have to forget about trying to get back to England. The German borders are too tight. None of the escapers are getting through." That wasn't quite true; out of the hundreds who had tried, two airmen had succeeded in making it home — but the odds against it were mountainous.

"But there could be something better than staying here. My home isn't far from here." Joe's native hearth was in Czechoslovakia, just south of the Riesen Gebirge, the mountain range that divided the old Czechoslovakia from Germany.

"There are lots of prisoners working in that area — enlisted men — most of them from Stalag 8B at Lamsdorf. They are in working parties contracted out to factories and farms in Czechoslovakia — sugarbeet factories and the like.

"If we could get on one of those working parties, we could make connections with my own backyard. It may not get us back to Britain right away, but at least we could sit out the war somewhere in Bohemia. There are plenty of folks who'd help us there."

It sounded good, I said, but how would two officers go about getting on a working party alongside other-ranks prisoners from Lamsdorf?

"That's not difficult," said Joe. "We trade places with a couple of enlisted men — at the big POW hospital in Lamsdorf. All we have to do is get ourselves into that hospital." Lamsdorf was the site of the central hospital serving most of the Allied prison camps in Germany. It was adjacent to the huge Wehrmacht other-ranks camp of Stalag 8B.

"Sure, Joe, but it's not that easy getting into the hospital. What happens to be wrong with us?"

"There has to be something," said Joe, grinning again. "After all, I do have a hernia. Yeah, a real one. Got kicked by the Gestapo when they were interrogating me in Warsaw. Jesus, you must have something. Everybody has something wrong with them. Anyway, let's go and see Doc Monteuis. He might have an idea or two."

Dr. Edward Monteuis was the only physician, and often surgeon, in Stalag Luft 3. A major in the Royal Army Medical Corps, he had been taken prisoner when the Germans overran the Scottish 51st Division at St. Valery during the Dunkirk debacle in 1940. Dr. Monteuis (pronounced Montwee) was a Scotsman from Edinburgh whose French-sounding name harked back to the long centuries of the French-Scottish alliance against the English.

He was a good soldier, a cheerful fellow prisoner, an entertaining companion and a fanatical bridge player. Above all, he was a good doctor. He ministered not only to our physical needs but, like every good physician, to our mental and psychological ones as well.

It was pretty hard to convince any POW that he was lucky to be behind the barbed wire, but Dr. Monteuis gave it a good try.

"Stop your moaning, you chaps!" he would say from time to time. "Some day you're going to be glad you were here. A year in this place could add ten years to your life.

"Don't you see, there's no danger of your over-eating." (That was a sick joke, but we laughed all the same.) "You're slim and trim with no unhealthy blubber, and you're not smoking the way you used to — and getting plenty of fresh air." (There were plenty of broken windows in the barracks, which the Germans never found time to mend.)

"And think of the sleep you're getting. That rest is important. It will stand you in good stead later in life. And you're not boozing it up with the girls until three o'clock in the morning the way you did back on squadron. Believe me, chaps, this is the best thing ever happened to you!"

We became quite fond of Dr. Monteuis. He was always telling us the things we liked to hear. Some of the prisoners, notably the British public-school types, made a regular discipline of suffering an ice-cold shower in the washroom every day. Dr. Monteuis didn't think much of that.

"Forget that 'cleanliness is next to godliness' stuff," he would tell us. "In a place like this you are better off with a nice, thick film of greasy dirt next to your skin — protects you against the cold!"

But for all his comforting geniality, he could be a bit of a stickler when it came to professional decorum. One of the most common ailments in the camp was a painful and distressing inflammation of the upper and inner thighs, a condition that the boys described, rather aptly, as crotch rot.

Dr. Monteuis detested that label. On sick parade one morning he made that quite clear.

"I don't ever want to hear that word *crotch rot* again, do you hear? Never again. I shall refuse to treat any man who uses the word. The condition is medically known as *tinea cruris*. Get that? *Tinea cruris*. Anyone calling it anything else won't get treated. That's final!"

Tinea cruris, of course, would hardly qualify anyone for transfer to the big hospital at Lamsdorf. For the purpose Joe had in mind we needed an ailment that Dr. Monteuis might normally refer to the better-equipped clinic.

We found Dr. Monteuis in a good mood. He had just finished a bit of minor surgery, in which he had sought to put his patient at ease with his inimitable brand of humour. The patient had come to him with an angry red boil on the back of his neck.

"Dear, dear," said the doctor, "that's bad, isn't it? Must do something about that, mustn't we? Well, just step over here by the window. I can't see very well at the best of times, and we need all the light we can get. That's better. Oh, dear, that is a nasty boil, isn't it? This is going to hurt. Afraid all I have is this old razor blade, old chap. Not very sharp, either. Bit rusty, too. Ah, well, do the best we can, won't we?"

The patient, of course, didn't believe a word of it. Doc Monteuis's running commentaries during an "operation" came to be regarded as his substitute for an anaesthetic.

Joe came quickly to the point. We wanted to get into the hospital at Lamsdorf, and could Dr. Monteuis provide us with an authentic excuse.

"Oh, dear . . . Let me see . . . well, you do have that hernia, Ricks? It's not bothering you much, is it? But then, who's to say? Yes, it's my professional opinion that we should have a specialist look at it. Fair enough! But as for you, Brown, what's wrong with you?"

I could only remind him that a few months previously I had complained to him of an annoying sign of hemorrhoids. It was a common complaint with new prisoners. The German diet of barley, black bread and potatoes played havoc with more delicate intestinal tracts.

"Ah, yes, so you did. Gave you some salve, didn't I? Do any good?"

"It helped a bit, Doc. But I still have a lot of itching."

"Oh, dear, I'm afraid there's not much more I can do for you, is there? After all, my resources here are pretty limited. Perhaps we'd better let those good surgeons up at Lamsdorf have a look at you. Very well, boys, I'll put you down for Lamsdorf."

Two weeks later we were on the train to Lamsdorf. It was an uneventful journey. We were escorted to the hospital where a Wehrmacht captain, a little white-haired gentleman of an age that clearly prohibited front-line service, looked us over carefully and checked our identities, made some copious notes in some kind of ledger and turned us over to a British orderly who showed us to the common ward where we would make our stay.

It was a week or more before the medical staff could find time to see us. They were much too busy. The hospital had just received a batch of seriously wounded prisoners from the Italian front and still had on its hands a number of amputees who had come in earlier from North Africa and were not convalescing.

We had plenty of time to hear their stories. One of the amputees, minus a leg, was a lad of about twenty who had been a worker in the Ford Motor

Company plant at Dearborn, Michigan, before he joined the U.S. Army tank corps. He was in remarkably good cheer and happy to be alive.

"You know, I'm never going to believe the newspapers again," he said. "Back home I used to read all that stuff about how the Jerries killed their prisoners. Jeez, I really believed it. Yeah, and I heard it on the radio, too.

"We were in a Sherman, in Tunisia, just rolling along nicely when we topped a little hill and there was a German Tiger straight ahead of us, coming our way. I don't know who saw who first, but we got off the first shot. The goddamn shell was a direct hit, right on the turret — and bounced off! Goddamn thing just bounced off — and then the Tiger fired, and that's all I remember.

"When I came to I was stretched out on the sand, and a little ways off the Sherman was burning. And the Tiger was standing right by me, and this German was doing something to my leg. My leg was one hell of a mess and he was fixing a tourniquet on it.

"He could speak some English. Said he had to get going but he would radio back and tell them where I was, and pretty soon he said an ambulance would pick me up. Jeez, I couldn't believe it. But sure enough, I guess it was about a half-hour later one of these half-tracks with a big red cross on it came up and they took me away."

He kept shaking his head as in disbelief.

"They been awful good to me. Jeez, those goddamn newspapers. I'll never believe 'em again!"

A few cots away another one-legged soldier was resting. He was English, a lieutenant in the Sherwood Foresters Regiment from Field Marshal Montgomery's Eighth Army.

"Did a nice job on me here, didn't they?" He turned down the bedsheet to display what was left of his leg. It had been amputated just above the knee, and the stump now had a well-healed, clean, healthy appearance.

"Pretty nice, what?" A mischievous leer spread over his face, and he laughed. "Boy, just wait till my wife sees that — if that doesn't satisfy her, nothing will!"

There were no nurses in the Lamsdorf hospital. Nursing duties were undertaken by a staff of orderlies, most of whom were other-ranks prisoners from the British Army. One of the more entertaining among them was a bright and energetic NCO from a Gurkha regiment attached to Montgomery's Eighth Army in Africa. Upon learning that two new patients had arrived and that they were officers, he was quick to present himself to us.

"Have the *sahibs* hunted tiger yet?" he inquired, in much the same tone as he might have asked of a new arrival at the officers' mess in Poona. I told him that we had not yet had that pleasure.

"Aha! It is indeed time you hunted tiger, *sahib*. All British officers hunt tiger. I have found tiger for many, many, many English officers. They know me. They know I am best tiger hunter in all of India. When do you want to hunt tiger?"

I had the impression that he was quite ready to

accompany me into the jungle that very day. I had to explain that I thought it would be better to wait until the war was over.

"Yes, yes, *sahib.* War soon over! You see! Now I give you my address in India. Just as soon as war over you come see me. I promise you fine tiger. Good tiger. Big tiger. But you not ask after other tiger men. You ask English officers. They tell you I am best tiger hunter in India. Good tiger, good price."

He was a good fellow, happy and enthusiastic. Every time I saw him bustling from bed to bed around the wards, I tried to imagine him seated beside me on top of an elephant as we pursued his "big tiger" through the jungles of Bengal. Nobody had ever invited me to a tiger hunt before. I felt flattered; it gave me an upper-crust Sandhurst feeling. I had met so many nice people in Germany, even tiger hunters.

Our names finally turned up on the treatment roster. The medics didn't think much of Joe Ricks's hernia; they furnished him with a simple truss and told him to avoid lifting heavy weights. My case was handled by a young Canadian medical officer, a Dr. Green from the Essex Scottish Regiment, who had been taken prisoner at Dieppe in 1942. After consultation with one of the German staff, he elected to give me a single application of injection therapy, which happily cured my condition for the rest of my life.

The stage was set for our exchange enterprise. We had had ample time to find the two enlisted male patients from Stalag 8B who would swap iden-

tities with us. Joe was most fortunate in finding a
Czech compatriot who even co-operated to the
point of having the same flat features and stubby
nose as Joe. I found my alias in Sergeant Alfred
Taylor, an air gunner in the Royal Air Force, a London Cockney who was only too happy to get a
chance to sample what he imagined to be the *dolce
vita* at the officers' camp in Sagan.

On discharge from hospital Joe and I were
delivered without incident to Stalag 8B, while two
instant flight lieutenants, miraculously fitting into
the uniforms of Brown and Ricks, went off by train
to Stalag Luft 3, some 150 kilometres to the west.

> *Oh, what a tangled web we weave,*
> *When first we practice to deceive!*

I never fully understood that quote until after
we had arrived at the other-ranks camp at Lamsdorf. Everything had started out so well. We were
both elated. We had been so clever and had outwit-
ted the enemy. It had been indeed "a piece of
cake." Everything augured well for the success of
our operation. But it turned out other than we had
expected.

For several days we basked in our status as
rather mysterious newcomers among the denizens
of Stalag 8B. This dirty, depressing, sprawling
metropolis of fifty thousand was a far cry from Hermann Göring's guest-house for Allied officer aircrew at Stalag Luft 3. The population was compos-
ed mostly of thousands of British from the summer
of Dunkirk, but there were also hundreds of Cana-

dian boys, shackles on their wrists, who had been captured at Dieppe, and Palestinians from the Jewish battalions who had fallen into Rommel's hands at Tobruk.

Then the blow fell.

It was midmorning, on our fourth day in Lamsdorf, when we had the shock of hearing our names broadcast over the elaborate public-address system that reached every corner of the camp. There was a loudspeaker mounted at every street intersection.

"Attention! Attention! Flight Lieutenant Brown and Flight Lieutenant Ricks. Report at once to the *Abwehr* [security] officer at the main gate. Attention! Flight Lieutenant Brown and Flight Lieutenant Ricks. Report at once . . .''

At fifteen-minute intervals throughout the morning, the message echoed monotonously through the miles of dingy barracks. We were dumbfounded. We couldn't understand what could possibly have gone wrong. All four of us had spent long hours in the hospital learning each other's identities. We were so sure we had attained perfection in the business of being people we were not.

Only much later did we learn what had gone wrong. We had overlooked one small detail; we had not told our exchange pair the number of our barrack block back at Stalag Luft 3. The ersatz Brown and Ricks had been tripped up the moment they entered the camp at Sagan.

What should be done?

In that vast camp of 50,000 we might easily have gone into hiding. But the prisoners' Man of

Confidence, a Dutch-Canadian warrant officer, advised against it.

"No dice! You'll have to turn yourselves in. If you don't, they are going to come in after you. There will be a mass search. They don't do that often; it's too difficult for them. But with two officers on the loose they won't be taking any chances.

"And right now we can't risk a mass search. We already have two or three of our boys in hiding. One of them is a kid who was out on a working party and tossed a piece of chain into the turbine of a power plant. If they find him they'll hang him. We can't risk it. I'm sorry, but you'll just have to surrender. Tough luck!"

We saw his point.

We marched down to the main gate and asked to see the *Abwehr* officer. A few minutes later a Wehrmacht major was peering at us through the barbed wire. He was laughing at us.

"You don't fool me. You're not Brown and Ricks!"

We insisted we were, but the *Abwehr* man kept on shaking his head and grinning.

"I'm not a fool," he said. "Look, there are two British officers loose in that camp. They had some purpose in coming here — they went to a lot of trouble. You think they are going to surrender the minute we ask for them? *Nichts!*"

He turned his back on us while we were still talking, and for the rest of the day the loudspeakers at the intersections blasted their demand that Brown and Ricks report to the main gate.

We were back at the main gate the next morning. The Man of Confidence was getting jittery and urging haste upon us. He was terrified lest the Germans start to mount their mass search. They would tear the camp apart, he said. It would jeopardize their escape organization and uncover the fugitive prisoners.

This time we had some limited success. The *Abwehr* major told the guard to unlock the gate and then led us straight to the cooler, the big brick-and-concrete building that housed the solitary confinement cells. But he was not convinced that we were Brown and Ricks.

"*Verstehen Sie*, I don't know who you are. I don't care much either. We'll find out sooner or later. All I do know is that you are not Brown and Ricks. They are still in the camp. But we'll find them, we'll find them. *Das ist bestimmt!*"

There then ensued eleven days of the most grotesque comedy I have ever known. The punishment block at Stalag 8B was pure Alice in Wonderland. It was not at all like the cooler back at Stalag Luft 3. There the solitary confinement cells were precisely that — places for hard arrest and solitary confinement. Here at Lamsdorf the punishment block had all the disorderly charm of a stevedores' poker club.

The cell doors were always open except during the occasional perfunctory inspection by the orderly officer. The inmates spent most of their time congregated in the big furnace room, where they were presided over by a big, handsome, good-natured former Yorkshire coal miner who was the de facto supervisor of the block. The cells were primarily for sleeping, or for uninterrupted games of chess.

Our major domo of the block, like so many of the others, had been taken at Dunkirk in 1940. He was now a permanent fixture in the cooler. But for the indulgence of an understanding *Kommandant*, he ought to have been doing a ten-year stretch of hard labour in the notorious Wehrmacht military prison at Fort Zinna. For that had been his sentence when a military court had found him guilty of illicit sexual intercourse with a German girl, contrary to the Nazi blue law. It had happened while he was out on a working party.

"It was just that her boyfriend was jealous," he said. "They had us doing construction work on an air base, and she was on the office staff. Her boyfriend was a Luftwaffe corporal. The only thing that worries me now is if my old lady back in Yorkshire ever finds out about it. What do you think? Will they ever know about this back at home?"

I told him not to worry. War concealed a multitude of sins. I told him the story about the Czech fighter pilot who was shot down by his jealous flight commander. I think it made him feel better.

"Anyway," I said, "your wife will be so damn happy to have you home again she wouldn't give a damn even if she did find out — but she won't!"

But that first evening in the furnace room our own anxieties had birth. We had just finished explaining to our new friends why we were here, and who we were, when a lean, haunted-looking individual emerged from the group to confront us.

"That's *Namentausch!*" he said. "You switched names. *Namentausch!* Now you've gone and done it. You wait and see. Look at me. That's what I did. Now I've been here a year and gone, all for *Namentausch.* You'll be here for the rest of your life. You'll see!"

He was quite agitated.

"Once you start on that road there's no end to it," he went on. "After a while you'll forget who you really are. Yes, you will! Look, I've been everything. I've been a Frenchman and I've been a Dane. I think originally I was a Cypriot. But then I became a Romanian Jew. Now nobody knows who I am. And the Germans don't seem to care anymore. They just leave me here. They don't even talk to me anymore.

"So they got you for *Namentausch*, eh? You'll be sorry. You probably thought you were real clever, just like I did. But you'll be sorry."

I began to feel a little nervous.

On the orderly officer's next visit we asked to see the *Abwehr* officer again, and a little later we were paraded into his office. He was quite pleasant and smiled throughout the interview. It was a sarcastic smile.

"Look, boys, I don't know what those two officers in there are up to. Sooner or later we'll find out. But whatever it is, they wouldn't be likely to surrender as easily as you did. Nothing doing!"

At this point Joe broke in.

"But, *mein Herr*, when we came to the hospital there was a *Hauptmann* who checked us in. He had white hair. He would remember us."

The major looked surprised. He made a call on the telephone, and about an hour later we were once more called out of the punishment block and paraded into the *Abwehr* office. The white-haired *Hauptmann* was there. He studied us carefully — frontal view, side view, quarter view. He then turned to the *Abwehr* major and shook his head.

"*Nein!* I never saw these men before in my life!"

Back in the furnace room our Cypriot friend nodded in gloomy sympathy.

"What did I tell you, eh? You're going to be here with me forever. Say, either of you fellows play chess?"

A couple of German guards dropped into the furnace room that evening, and a big poker game was abandoned in favour of a spirited discussion about the authenticity of werewolves and the magic of *Walpurgis Nacht*. The Germans were solid, peasant types who, it was evident, pretended to be not at all superstitious. They seemed to enjoy their visits to the furnace room, probably because the inmates invariably had good American cigarettes from their Red Cross parcels.

It was during the talk about werewolves that I had my inspiration. Joe was back in his cell, and I interrupted him in the middle of a chess game with the Cypriot.

"Joe! Fingerprints! Remember? Back in Sagan

they have our fingerprints. Why didn't we think of that?"

Joe snorted. "Why the hell didn't *they* think of it? Stupid bastards! Some *Abwehr!*"

We couldn't wait for morning to ask to see the *Abwehr* major. For once he stopped smiling.

"Bestimmt! Fingerabdrucken! Come with me!"

Ten minutes later we were back in the furnace room washing the ink off our fingers and wondering how long it would take the fingerprints to get back to Sagan and win our release. It was not long; two days later we were marched out of the punishment block and paraded this time before the *Kommandant* himself. He was flanked by both the *Abwehr* man and his adjutant. All three spoke close to perfect English.

We were formally on charge, we were told.

The offence: *Namentausch.* Did we have anything to say before judgement was passed? These Germans made such an effort to be what they considered *korrekt.*

Common sense dictated that we let the hearing take its course. There was obviously no defence. But occasions of drama were such rare and welcome breaks in the even tenor of a prisoner's life that the temptation to make the most of it was irresistable.

"You have no jurisdiction, *mein Herr.*"

I was now no longer an air force pilot and a prisoner of war. I was playing Clarence Darrow before the Supreme Court. The Walter Mitty in me

was having a field day. I was about to make history
in German military law.

"No jurisdiction?" said the adjutant. He looked
and sounded incredulous.

"No, *mein Herr*. We are air force personnel. We
are under the personal protection of the *Reichsmarschall*, Hermann Göring. The Wehrmacht has
no jurisdiction to try us."

It was sheer nonsense, of course, and I knew it,
but it put me in the centre of the stage and I was enjoying every second of it. Like most other people, I
like attention.

The *Kommandant* looked perplexed and turned
to the adjutant. He in turn, a little flustered now,
grabbed at a big volume that looked very like our
own *King's Rules and Regulations* and sifted nervously through the pages. Then he looked up in
frustration.

"That doesn't seem to be covered here. Gentlemen, we shall have to refer your case to the judge
advocate general, in Berlin." The court was
adjourned.

Back in the cooler Joe turned on me angrily.
"You stupid, goddamn smart aleck! What the hell
did you do that for? Now we'll be here for weeks
while the bureaucrats debate the case in Berlin.
Hell, they would only have given us fifteen days in
any case. You bloody idiot!" For a Czech in the RAF
he had picked up idiomatic English quickly.

I told him I was sorry. What with chess, poker
and endless philosophy in the furnace room,
always in a fog of tobacco smoke, the time passed

quickly enough. It was only days before we were summoned once more to the *Kommandantur*. The adjutant seemed smugly pleased.

"It has been determined by the judge advocate general that our military law applies to all branches of the armed forces, yours as well as ours. You are within our jurisdiction."

This time I had nothing to say.

"The sentence is fifteen days' hard arrest and solitary confinement. But we are sending you back to your own camp. You will serve your sentence there."

That was too much. The prospect of doing solitary back at Stalag Luft 3, with no furnace room, no Yorkshire major domo, no chess or poker or evening socials with the guards was altogether too forbidding. I couldn't help myself; I had to be Clarence Darrow again.

"But, *mein Herr*, we have already served eleven days of solitary here in Stalag 8B."

The *Kommandant* frowned, pursed his lips, looked at his adjutant and then shrugged his shoulders and smiled.

"Give them a receipt for eleven days," he said.

The receipt was honoured at Stalag Luft 3, but I had already learned my lesson. Never again would I be guilty of *Namentausch.* The case of the Cypriot still haunts me. Unlike so many others, I am satisfied that I have found my identity, and I am quite happy with it. I don't want any other.

And I have kept that receipt for eleven days, just to fortify my resolution. It has become one of my prized possessions.

XI

A Christmas in the Cooler

We changed trains at Breslau on the journey home to Sagan. It was late afternoon and the guards decided that it was time for a meal. They guided us along the platform to the German Red Cross canteen at the far end of the station. A prominent sign over the entrance proclaimed that the place was *"Nur für Wehrmacht"* — for armed forces only. Before we left Lamsdorf our officers' battledress tunics had been returned to us, and we were conscious of the attention we received as we entered the canteen. The "Canada" flash on my shoulder was almost burning.

The restaurant was crowded.

There was nothing that remotely resembled the parade ground. A train had just pulled in from the east, bringing its cargo of battle-weary men from the *Ostfront*, from the chilling misery in the blood-spattered snows of Staraya Russa, the Ilmensee and the Dnieper bridgeheads. These were men who since Stalingrad and Kursk had tasted only a bitter string of defeats at the hands of a now seemingly invincible Red Army. All the proud élan of 1941 and 1942 had been drained out of them, and they showed it.

Theirs were no longer the boyish faces of recruits impatient for the front. These were men hardened in the most gruelling military contest of modern times. They were still survivors, but the horrors of the Russian front had left their indelible mark. There was a uniform greyness in the men's complexions, and the faces of many of even the younger men were lined and drawn. Most of them appeared too weary even to indulge in the usual banter of off-duty servicemen.

We had to stand in line for five or ten minutes until one of the young, uniformed Red Cross women found places for us at one of the long tables. We were no sooner seated, and had just started on our bowls of soup, when there was a commotion in the centre aisle at the end of our table. A big, burly *Feldwebel* (sergeant), heavily laden with bedroll, rifle and all the accoutrements of a front-line infantryman, was pointing at us and screaming in indignation.

It was not difficult for us to get the drift of what he was saying: "I'm a German soldier. I'm a fighting man from the *Ostfront*, and I have to stand and wait while you feed those *gottverdammte* baby-killing English terror bombers! You give a seat to air gangsters and make a good German soldier stand."

I was embarrassed. This was the kind of attention we could do without. I was also not a little alarmed. His rhetoric was so violent that I expected it might at any moment provoke the other troops in the place to throw us out and do us bodily harm.

It didn't happen. The *Feldwebel* was suddenly confronted by one of the *Rotes Kreuz* girls, possibly the canteen supervisor, who stepped up to him and told him sharply to "Shut up!"

The *Feldwebel* lowered his voice a little but continued his complaint, making frequent references to the fact that the canteen was supposed to be for armed forces only: "*Nur für Wehrmacht.*"

Then it happened. It was an impressive demonstration of the pervasive German respect for authority. The *Feldwebel* made no resistance as the Red Cross girl grabbed him by an elbow, twisted him around and marched him to the door of the canteen. Just before she pushed him out onto the platform we heard her final words:

"They're soldiers, too. *Raus!* Get out!"

It was getting dark when we boarded the train to Sagan. We found seats in one of the large third-

class compartments. It was several days before
Christmas, and the train was packed with people
going happily on their way home to spend the holiday with friends and family. In our compartment
were three young women who turned out to be
schoolteachers, a lean, sallow member of the Hitler
Youth in his uniform, and a friendly *Wehrmacht* officer, a major, going home minus a leg. He had left
it somewhere on the Russian front.

After I had chatted with the major for a while, I
couldn't resist asking him why he wasn't travelling
first class. He laughed and pointed to the wings insignia on my jacket.

"No first-class cars on this train — you smashed
them all up!"

Except for the tiny blue blackout lamp, the
compartment was in darkness. The guards were in
a genial mood and had no objection to our convers-
ing with the other passengers. My "Canada"
flashes seemed to draw the most attention, and I
sensed that Canada held a certain fascination for
Germans generally. One of the schoolteachers said
she knew a young man who was now a prisoner of
war in Canada. There had been letters from him,
she said. He was being treated well and had even
written that he would like to stay in Canada after
the war. It was the kind of thing we liked to hear,
and I thought the other passengers looked on us
more kindly after hearing it.

After we had talked for a while, someone began
to sing — I think it was one of the schoolteachers. It
was a folk song of some kind, and some of the
others joined in. Then one of them asked if we had a

song. A little self-consciously I sang *Bombay Troopship* and what I could remember of *Alouette;* then, to vaunt my knowledge of German, I gave them the first verse of *Lili Marlene: "Bei der Kaserne, bei dem grossen Tor!"* The first verse was all I knew. Everyone smiled and applauded.

Joe got off a Czech folk song or two, which got him into conversation with one of the schoolteachers whose home was in the Sudeten country. After that the three girls led the rest of us in singing Christmas carols.

"Silent Night, Holy Night . . ." The snow-draped forest slipped by us in the darkness as we sang. We forgot we were prisoners. The German officer seemed to have forgotten the leg he had lost in Russia. For all of us that evening the war seemed to have gone away. We talked of families and children, happy Christmases gone and happier ones to come.

It was a brief, exquisitely beautiful hour of comradeship and is my most treasured memory of Germany. In that hour there were no guards and prisoners, nor any foes. In that delicately suspended hour we were humbly happy human beings enjoying the songs of our childhood. Under the gentle, warm spell of Christmas the Spirit of Man was paramount.

When we left the train at Sagan, we bumped into Hans Pieber on the platform. Captain Pieber was on the administrative staff of Stalag Luft 3. He was an Austrian who had never shown any great enthusiasm for National Socialism and frequently revealed the direction of his loyalties by providing prisoners with such subversive contraband as maps and photographic paper. Pieber was also supervisor of the *Kommandantur* censorship department, which scrutinized both the incoming and outgoing mail of all prisoners.

He hadn't come to the station to meet us; he was probably off on Christmas leave to his home in Vienna. But he stopped long enough to greet me:

"Welcome home, Herr Brown! And how's the Rose of Nova Scotia?"

I gaped at him in surprise and suddenly realized the extent to which our captors kept us under surveillance. Out of sheer whimsy I had frequently addressed letters to my wife in Canada with the subscript "The Rose of Nova Scotia." I was astonished to find that even this unimportant bit of fancy had become part of enemy intelligence.

Under the Geneva Convention prisoners were permitted to correspond with next of kin and others to a limit of three letters and four postcards a month. Both the enemy and our own intelligence branches kept sharp watch over every line of correspondence and also used the prisoner-of-war mail themselves to further their own intelligence purposes. Through an elaborate coding system, the prisoners' organization was able to transmit a vast amount of information about conditions in Germany back to London.

The Germans, for their part, used POW mail in other ways. One startling evidence of this came to light in Stalag Luft 3 when one of the British prisoners received a letter from a woman in Oxford, England. It was couched in most affectionate and

intimate terms and dealt chattily with affairs of obviously mutual knowledge. His name on the envelope, as well as his rank, his serial number and even
his POW number, were accurate.

Yet he had never heard of this woman in his
life.

He turned the letter over to the camp intelligence group, which in turn reported the case to the
appropriate office in London. The result, as we
learned much later, was the arrest of a German
female agent in Oxford. Her letter, of course, was a
coded message, meant to be intercepted by German intelligence and not delivered to Stalag Luft 3.
A compatriot's negligence cost that woman her life.

Joe and I spent Christmas in the cooler. It was
not a bit like the punishment block at Lamsdorf. In
Stalag Luft 3 solitary confinement meant exactly
that. Each man was locked into a small cell just
large enough to accommodate a narrow wooden
bunk, a small table and a chair. The walls, like the
floor, were of bare concrete. The small window high
on one wall was barred, and a boxlike wooden con-
traption on the outside, while admitting light and
air, blocked off any view of the world beyond. The
door was a single steel plate with the usual
peephole.

The Sagan cooler had nothing of the social
warmth of the furnace room at Lamsdorf, and I was
happy that our receipt from Stalag 8B had been
honoured here and that we had only the four days'
solitary to serve. There wasn't even time to do any
serious reading. On my previous session in solitary,
after the abortive escape with Gordon Brettell, I had

sent for all five volumes of Macaulay's *History of England* and passed the fifteen days to advantage.

The prospect of spending Christmas in the cooler was a bit disheartening. Christmas in the camp compound couldn't be anything like Christmas at home, but it was at least a cheerful simulation. There had always been the usual binge on our own rather poisonous distilled spirits, and for our previous Christmas there had been a gift of several truckloads of kegged beer, which, the *Kommandant* explained, came with the best wishes of the *Reichsmarschall*, Hermann Göring.

Christmas morning, 1943, brought nothing but the sight of four bare concrete walls and the prospect of the usual trip to the *Wäscheraum* for a shave, followed by the usual "hard arrest" rations for the day.

But there was a surprise.

There had been the usual breakfast of black bread, a piece of margarine and a dab of ersatz jam, and a mug of chickory, but then a little later the door had opened again and one of the guards beckoned me out into the passageway. He had already called on Joe, who was standing by him grinning. The guard put a finger to his lips and gave us a wink, and then led us along the corridor to the orderly room.

Several of the guards, all NCOs, were lounging around the room. One of their number stood at the window next to the door to the outside. Our guard nodded his head in his direction and told us that we must be careful lest "some officer dropped around."

I couldn't think why we were here and felt somewhat ill at ease standing in the middle of the orderly room. There seemed to be an inexplicable air of expectancy. The guards were looking at us in what I felt was something akin to amusement. Then one of them, the fellow sitting at the orderly room desk, reached out to the radio set in front of him and turned up the volume.

It was just in time to catch the inimitable and resonant majesty of Westminster's Big Ben. I could scarcely believe my ears. Every German in the room was grinning from ear to ear.

"This is London calling . . ."

It was the Christmas greeting from the king. And it was the gift of a half-dozen German soldiers to two other soldiers wearing a different uniform.

XII

Escape from the Bedbugs

My next escape adventure came in the summer of 1944, but it was not a genuine attempt to escape. It was an ersatz escape, a phony one, having nothing whatever to do with one's service duty but pursued solely in the interests of personal ease and comfort.

It was undertaken in the company of Gwyn Martin, who is today a respectable dispensing chemist in Aberystwyth, Wales. Gwyn is one of my brightest and happiest memories from Stalag Luft

3. He was a big-boned typical Welsh highlander, strong like an ox and terrifying on the football field. He had black eyes, black, undisciplined hair and a ruddy skin like beefsteak. When he laughed he shook the barracks, and when he sang, as every Welshman must as a matter of tribal instinct, it was like a cracked record of a noble Wagner overture.

Gwyn was a navigator in the RAF and part of the all-Welsh crew of a Wellington bomber. His pilot was Shag Rhys, who was shorter than Gwyn, but stockier, and just as tough. His friends said that from his appearance and deportment he was most certainly the reincarnation of a mad Druid priest. It must have been quite a crew.

One night early in 1942, they had raided a naval installation somewhere on the Norwegian coast. Their instruments had suffered some damage when they were hit by flak. A few hours later, on what ought to have been the flight home, Shag asked his navigator where they were.

"Damned if I know," said Gwyn cheerfully, and he didn't.

The weather was zero-zero, and after they had drawn a blank on the RDF (Radio Direction Finder) and had no more than fifteen minutes' fuel in the tanks, Rhys decided to let down slowly and ditch in the ocean. From his deadest kind of dead reckoning Gwyn figured they were somewhere over the North Sea.

It was surprisingly flat and calm. The Wellington hit the water nicely and sank in a matter of minutes. Unfortunately the life raft failed in its automatic discharge from its stowage, and the crew were left floundering around in the darkness, with only their Mae Wests to keep them afloat.

All of them, that is, except Gwyn Martin, for he had characteristically left his Mae West hanging dry and tidy in his locker back at base. He swam around in the blackness for about twenty minutes, but in his heavy flying boots and flight jacket he quickly tired. The others heard his casual good-bye from out of the foggy darkness.

"So long, chaps. I'm done!"

But about five seconds later they heard him come back to life.

"Hey, chaps, I'm walking on the bottom!"

In the misty dawn they all walked ashore from the tiny lake, not much larger than a duck pond, deeply cradled in a narrow valley between steeply towering Norwegian mountains.

The good Lord, who concerns himself equally with the safety of sparrows, small children, drunkards and Welshmen, had led them through the mountains to the only spot within hundreds of miles where they could have put down the aircraft without being smashed into eternity. As Gwyn used to put it, "I don't think He was quite ready to face us!"

All of which explains how Gwyn came to join me at Stalag Luft 3. In the spring of 1944 we both found ourselves in a group being "purged" from the main Sagan camp to a new, auxiliary compound several miles away, a much smaller installation that went by the name of Fort Belaria.

Its *Kommandant* boasted that Belaria was escape-proof, and so, when it opened for business, its original complement was largely selected from those old prisoners in the main camp who had persistently snubbed the *Reichsmarschall* by excusing themselves from his hospitality. In this purge to Belaria Gwyn and myself were included.

I had found by this time that among prisoners of war there were, generally speaking, three principal topics of conversation. These were, in order of priority, the war, food and women. At Belaria, however, we quickly uncovered another topic of peak priority — bedbugs, or, as they came to be known in the bitter and voluminous correspondence with the Germans, *Bettwanzen.*

They were small insects and, to begin with, not very numerous, so for several months they were actually welcomed as something of a wryly humorous distraction from the rather sordid monotony of prison routine. There were bedbug races, solemn bedbug executions and contests to see who could slaughter the most bugs at any given time — all activities of signal service in preserving camp morale and our precapture levels of sanity.

With the advent of warmer weather, however, the novelty wore off. Succeeding protests flowing from the senior Allied officer to the *Kommandant* were of increasingly indignant tone. When these failed to bring redress, the Swiss Commission was advised and a formal protest laid before the International Red Cross in Geneva.

The German action, when it came, was an indifferent program of fumigation. The big, ramshackle wooden barracks were impossible to make airtight; while the old-fashioned sulfur candles left the camp coughing and choking for days, they seemed to give the bedbugs a new zest for their nightly hunting in the bunks.

From that time forward the ascendancy was with the bugs. Their numbers increased in stagger-ing geometric progression. During the earlier spring months they had attacked singly or in pairs; now they invaded us nightly in division strength. You could actually hear them on the march, hear the repulsive plop, plop, plop as new arrivals parachuted down to the bunks from the ceilings where they bivouacked.

There was only token defence. The darkness after lights-out was broken by the sporadic flaring of matches, as one man after another sought to rout at least one of the marauders with flame. But it was useless, and the futility was emphasized by the pro-fanity that punctuated the long, itching torment of summer nights. A good night's sleep had become a memory, sweet but faint.

It was when our misery had reached its un-bearable zenith that Gwyn Martin was suddenly in-spired. It was on a hot day in late August. I remember that because our underground radio had just flashed the news that the Allies had taken Paris.

Gwyn and I had had a stroke of luck that day. We had been cultivating the acquaintance of a young guard by the name of Horst Reuter, a kid of about eighteen. He was a nice, bright boy doing guard duty while waiting to start flight training in the Luftwaffe, and he didn't drink. He had a girlfriend in Sagan. She was fond of chocolate, of which the Third Reich had none. Since we had some Red Cross chocolate bars, and Horst had only that day received his monthly ration of a litre of brandy, he thought that perhaps we would care to swap two chocolate bars for his bottle.

We took the bottle to a moderately secluded spot in a corner of the *Sportsplatz*, lay down in the sunshine and drank the brandy. It was very pleasant taking turns at the bottle. On the other side of the barbed wire we could see girls in fresh, bright print dresses pedalling their bikes along the highway. German fighters from the nearby aerodrome circled lazily overhead. The sun was warm, the breeze cool, the brandy brave and stirring, and it was good to be alive.

"Do you know," said Gwyn, "I know a place where there aren't any bedbugs."

"Sure, back home," I said.

"No. Right here in this camp. And I think we can get ourselves a bunk there."

"Go on," I said. I was watching a pretty blonde *Dienstmädel* walking along the highway on the arm of a Luftwaffe man. I felt tenderly for them.

"Yeah," said Gwyn. "In the cooler. All we have to do is get there."

We had both had our share of solitary confinement. We knew what those cells were like. Those clean, concrete walls could never harbour a bedbug. The cells would be cool and quiet.

"I never did get to read Gibbon's *Decline and Fall of the Roman Empire*," I said. "So how are we going to get into the cooler?"

"Easy," said Gwyn. "We'll fake an escape."

"We might get shot."

"Anything's better than bedbugs," said Gwyn. "But we can play this one dead safe. We could fix it with Paul so he'd be the one to nab us in the act."

Paul Reemt-Heeren was a special guard working for the camp security section. He was what we called a ferret, a sort of house dick in the prison camp. It was his duty to smell out subversive activities and stop escapes before they could happen.

Paul was a friend. He lives in Emden, West Germany, now, and I have occasionally heard from him. At Belaria he made life considerably easier and more comfortable both for Gwyn and me, and just incidentally for himself, by engaging in black market operations in such innocent items as onions, garlic, wine, lighter fluid and coal bricks for our stove. He took in exchange cans of Borden's Sweetened Condensed Milk, Lucky Strike cigarettes, chocolate bars and any other Red Cross issue that came our way.

We found Paul late that afternoon. He was dispiritedly poking about the camp incinerator with the special long iron rod he used for exploring suspected areas where something might be hidden. He was visibly depressed.

"I haven't had any leave since the invasion of France," he said. "I went to see the *Kommandant* this morning. I told him about my family. They were bombed out of our house. My wife and the four kids were evacuated to Magdeburg. I just want to see how they are fixed there, how they're living. I know they're having a pretty rough time.

"But the *Kommandant* says no leave . . . When is this *verdammte* war going to end, anyway?"

"Three weeks," we told him cheerfully.

Paul regarded us sourly.

"Like hell, three weeks. It'll take us longer than that to throw you bastards back into the Channel again!"

"Sure, sure," we said good-naturedly. It's a shame to kick a guy when he's down. Paul knew only too well what the war score was, and there was no sense rubbing it in.

"All I want is just a day or two. Just long enough to see what kind of a joint they're living in. That's not too much to ask. But that *Kommandant . . .*" Paul shook his head.

I looked at Gwyn. I thought I could hear the gears grinding beneath his shaggy scalp, just as I was sure he must have heard mine. If ever the moment were tactically right, this was it.

"Paul," I said, "do you suppose the *Kommandant* might listen to you if you were to find a tunnel, or a radio set, or catch a couple of prisoners escaping, something like that?"

That, said Paul, was just about the only way a man might get leave at Belaria. The *Kommandant* was like that — kept his troops in line with incentives.

"Why? What do you mean?" His eyes narrowed and he looked at us sharply.

We told him quickly of our plan. It would be a nice way to get him his leave. Once or twice he looked nervously over his shoulder as we talked. He was a bit doubtful at first; then he warmed up a bit; then just as quickly he showed puzzlement and suspicion.

"What's the game? What are you going to get

out of it?" Paul was a practical fellow. A security guard in a prison camp had to be.

We told him: fifteen days in the cooler, with no bedbugs and plenty of quiet reading time. Paul looked a little shocked at that. He said he had no idea the bedbugs were that bad. He said he had never known any bedbugs.

It all went according to plan.

Each evening at nine o'clock, the grounds of the compound were cleared of all prisoners and the barrack doors locked. Around 8:30 on the evening following our chat with Paul, we sauntered over to the wash-house, a brick structure standing next to the outside wire, and busied ourselves with the pretence of scrubbing our socks, until shortly before nine the few remaining prisoners had left for their barracks.

Once the wash-house was deserted, we shinnied up some pipes by the wall and pushed open the trapdoor that led to a low loft above. The trap had been placed there so that the overhead piping might be inspected or repaired. We pushed the trapdoor back in place and settled down to wait for Paul to make his appointed round.

"Might as well eat a little of our escape rations right now," said Gwyn with a laugh. "In a few minutes they are going to take it all away from us anyway."

We had equipped ourselves to pass for reasonable facsimiles of escape-bound prisoners. Our pockets were stuffed with a few Red Cross chocolate bars, some hard biscuits and other assorted odds and ends of food. We had also pocketed a dog-eared map of the German State Railways, as well as a plan of the Danzig dock area, an escape chart so common that virtually every prisoner had one. A few German banknotes added to the authenticity of the venture.

Paul arrived on schedule, and we set up the prearranged stomping and scuffling that was to be his cue to investigate. We made such a racket, in fact, that we learned later it was heard in half the barracks around the compound.

Paul's acting was superb.

When we pushed aside the hatch and peered down from the trap he was standing below us with a flashlight in one hand and his automatic pistol in the other. His eyes were flashing and his face flushed with excitement.

"Kommen Sie heraus!" he roared.

There was a grim menace in the beckoning gesture of the automatic, and for several apprehensive seconds I trembled at the thought that Paul might try to make a fake escape appear to be a real one by strewing a couple of corpses around.

"Komm'... komm'."

We went quietly.

Paul walked along behind us with the automatic pointed at our backs. We went through the centre of the compound, with hundreds of wondering eyes looking at us from the barrack windows, and then out through the main gate to the guardhouse.

At the guardhouse they stripped and searched us. While they were doing that, the *Kommandant* arrived and Paul had to tell his story. Once I looked at him while he was talking, but I quickly looked away because when he saw me looking at him he seemed to bite his lip to keep from laughing.

But even if he had laughed, I don't think it would have mattered much. The *Kommandant* was so excited he was only catching every fourteenth word. He kept glancing at Gwyn and me, then back at Paul again, and his face was a glowing mask of joy and triumph. He kept bringing his hands together so that the fingertips of one hand caressed the tips of the other, and his lips were pursed in a serene grimace of satisfaction.

After Paul had finished his story, the *Kommandant* went over to the table and fished around among the odds and ends they had taken from our pockets. Then he came across the map of the Danzig docks. He picked it up, chortled happily and turned on us with a smirk.

"You're a long, long way from Danzig, boys!" he jeered. He grinned benignly at the guards, and they grinned back at him, and nobody seemed to mind that we had joined in the grinning. Once again, as on that first night in Holland, I was reminded of a Rotary Club luncheon back at home.

"Give 'em their clothes and lock 'em up!"

I woke up next morning on the hard plank in the antiseptically spotless little concrete tank in the cooler. I yawned and stretched voluptuously and reflected how luxurious it was to live and sleep without bedbugs.

Very shortly, I knew, the guard would bring my

breakfast of mint tea and a slice of black bread, along with a basin and a jug of water so that I might wash.

And when he came, I would ask for pencil and paper so that I might write down a list of the books I would require for my fifteen days in solitary. I would ask for Gibbon's *Decline and Fall.* The prospect of undisturbed rest and quiet study in this pleasantly severe monastic setting gave me one of the most blissful moments I had known in years.

The key turned in the lock, and I jumped to my feet and readied myself to ask for the pencil and paper before the guard might get away from me.

The door opened. The guard was there, but he had no mint tea or bread.

"Put on your boots," he said.

I put on my boots, and he beckoned me into the corridor of the cell block and marched me to the orderly room. The *Feldwebel* in charge was listening to the *Deutschlandsender* and a dramatic account of how Germany's new rocket weapons were cutting the feet from under Eisenhower's assault on *Festung Europa.* London, it said, was already doomed.

Gwyn was already in the orderly room. The *Feldwebel* turned down the radio and looked at us with a superior grin.

"Such luck, such luck," he murmured. "We have such a pleasant *Kommandant.* He was so pleased this morning. Nobody yet has escaped from Belaria — that's why he is so pleased. He is so pleased he has sent word that you are not to be punished. Such luck!

"Schmidt! Take these officers back to their barracks!"

When we looked around the compound for Paul that morning he was nowhere to be found. A little later, when the sentries changed watch, we ran across Horst Reuter and asked him where Paul was.

"*Ach*, some people have all the luck! Paul's gone on leave. Five days. He's gone to see his family — took the train to Magdeburg this morning."

That night, while we lay sweating and scratching in our bunks, Gwyn struck a match, pursued a bedbug across his pillow and destroyed it with a sizzle and a pop.

"Do you know," he said, wistfully, "this is the first time in my life I think I've really had that feeling a Boy Scout is supposed to have when he has done his good deed for the day. Funny, isn't it?"

"I don't know," I said. "All I know is that the war is now almost over, and I shall never have another chance to get through Gibbon's *Decline and Fall.*"

And I never have.

XIII

Death March

Christmas of 1944 in Stalag Luft 3 was never better described than it was many years later by Kurt Vonnegut, Jr., in his World War II classic, *Slaughterhouse Five*.

The hero of that book was a U.S. infantryman taken prisoner by the Germans in the first hours of their last great offensive in the Ardennes, launched just before Christmas on December 16. The U.S. First Army was overrun, and the Germans herded their embarrassment of prisoners to the rear in the thousands. For want of space in their regular Wehrmacht camps, they thrust hundreds of them through the gates of Stalag Luft 3, the first time prisoners other than aircrew had graced our German home.

Vonnegut's description accurately describes the preparations we had made for what we hoped would be the last and best Christmas we celebrated behind the wire. Red Cross supplies had been coming through on a regular and generous basis during the preceding month or two. As Vonnegut faithfully recorded, we did indeed have a stock of literally millions of cigarettes and hundreds of thousands of chocolate bars.

Even better, we were able to present a full-dress gala performance of an old-time Christmas pantomime, with all the theatrical props and costumes the best Berlin costumier could supply. And the "leading lady" in the show, as *Slaughterhouse Five* records, was a blond and burly British public-school boy, late of a Spitfire squadron, who disgraced himself as the Blue Fairy Godmother by punching one of the new American arrivals in the jaw. Christmas '44 was all that Vonnegut said it was.

While the initial success of the German offensive had dampened our Christmas cheer to a degree, by New Year's Day we knew that the Germans' last push had run out of steam and that the Allies were on the march again. Over the ensuing weeks most of the U.S. Army prisoners had been transferred to other camps, but their bunks were quickly filled by incoming prisoners from the increasingly heavy night bombing operations of the RAF and the prodigious daylight raids by the U.S. Army Air Corps.

Then came the last week in January and the high drama of a winter morning when at last we heard the first faint promise of impending liberation.

We were on morning *Appell.* It was snowing. There was no wind, and the snow came down evenly and silently. In the customary manner, each barrack company stood at ease after it had been counted while the Germans went on to count the other groups. It was cold, and while we idly chatted we stamped our feet and clapped our hands to keep warm. Then someone shouted for silence.

"Listen! Shut up, you chaps! Listen!"

The chatter subsided.

In the near distance we could hear the *Feld-webel* perfunctorily counting heads in the adjoining ranks. But in the far distance there was something else.

"You hear that? Did you hear that?"

It was a rumbling, growling noise, and we knew it wasn't thunder. Sometimes it had the rolling sound of thunder, but it was periodically punctuated by a higher-pitched drumming of muffled blasts. The sound was east of us.

It was one of those moments filled with an almost unbearable kind of emotion. For a minute or so nobody said anything; then we were grabbing each other and slapping backs.

"The Russkies are coming, the Russkies are coming!" Somebody began to whistle the *Battle*

Hymn of the Republic, and I recall thinking what a fine sense of history he must have had.

On that same day the first trickle of refugees appeared, moving along the highway that flanked the barbed wire. Most of the traffic was in horse-drawn vehicles, loaded high with whatever these new dispossessed could bring with them. By the following morning the trickle had become a flood, and the horses and wagons were accompanied by people on foot. Women and children often sat on top of the baggage on the wagons, with old men and women bundled in blankets and shawls. As the stream of humanity thickened it became mingled with cattle.

These were no longer the refugees of earlier war years: the French, the Poles or the Russians. For the first time since war began, there were Germans on the move. In their tens of thousands, from East Prussia and the Polish frontier areas, they were fleeing in panic before the rapid advance of the Red Army.

By nightfall of the second day, our highway had become a stage for tragedy. Throughout the day we stood by the wire and watched the pitiful column of wagons, human beings and bawling cattle pushing painfully through the trampled, dirty snow. It had become much colder, and we could hear children crying from the piled-up heaps of baggage on the wagons.

All of us were conscious of the significance of what we were seeing. I don't think any of us escaped a sense that we were witnessing something in the nature of retribution. Germans were now suffering what Germans had caused others to suffer in earlier years. But we could not equate the crying children and the old men stumbling through the snow with those others who had sowed the harvest now being reaped.

At one point one of our number was moved to cry, in tones of exultation: "Good for 'em! They had it coming to 'em!"

The answer came instantly from a score of angry voices: "Shut up, you son of a bitch!"

It wasn't an hour for jubilation.

In the warmth and light of our huts that night, listening to the creaking of the wagon wheels, the shouts of weary men and the bawling of the cattle, few of us even dreamed that we might soon be joining that migration of misery. For most of us the sound of the Russian guns in the distance was an augury of imminent liberation. We did not imagine that the Germans had other plans for us.

They broke the news to us just before midnight.

An officer from the *Kommandantur* burst through the barrack door in a swirl of snowflakes. He stood in the doorway and bellowed at us. He was flushed and excited.

"We are evacuating the camp! Everybody must be ready to leave in half an hour. Put on all the warm clothing you have. We'll issue Red Cross parcels as you leave by the main gate. In half an hour!"

We stood stunned and silent for a moment after he had slammed the door behind him. Then the whole barrack erupted in a fever of activity. There were so many decisions to be made and so little time to make them; what to be taken, what to be left? Advice and counsel flew in every direction.

"Take the clothes with the most pockets . . . take extra socks . . . your feet could freeze . . . don't forget a newspaper . . . matches . . . paper is a good insulator, shove it in your jacket . . . never mind the bloody biscuits, too bulky . . . take all the chocolate bars you can lay your hands on.

"Cigarettes, boys, cigarettes. It's the only currency anybody in Germany is taking these days. Cigarettes are like gold."

And all the knitting of a thousand Red Cross circles back home suddenly came into its own. Balaclavas, toques, mittens and socks were now the prized items of dress.

It was a Canadian, rather logically, who hit on the idea of making sleds.

"There's a lot of snow out there, guys. We can take along a hell of a lot more gear and stuff if we haul it on sleds."

It was an idea whose time had come. In minutes every table and stool was being ripped apart and, with bed boards and other odds and ends, fashioned into crude but capable sleds. Belts and lengths of blanket cloth were twisted into harnesses. The few hammers in the block were in frantic demand, passed from hand to hand in the bedlam. In speedy negotiations prisoners formed themselves into units of two or three per sled, and the sleds were then piled high with cartons of cigarettes, remnants of Red Cross food, sometimes extra blankets.

Midnight came and went. From time to time a

German arrived from the *Kommandantur* to announce a brief postponement. It was a long night, but repeated postponements made possible a reasonable preparation for the ordeal.

Dawn was breaking when we were finally ordered out of the barracks. There was a light breeze, the snow was still falling, adding to the two-foot depth already on the ground, and it was icy cold. During the night the Germans had taken Red Cross food parcels from the stores, and the parcels were now piled in stacks by the main gate. As we marched out into the highway each man received an unopened parcel.

The civilian refugees were nowhere to be seen. A little later one of the Germans explained that the westward traffic was now under strict military control, with civilians restricted to certain roads and military formations to others. As we were soon to discover, we were sharing the highway with retreating units of the Germany army.

We were now part of what was to become known later as the Death March, the migration of tens of thousands of Allied prisoners across Germany, during the coldest days of winter, to prevent us from falling into the hands of the Russians. It was necessary, as the Germans explained to us, to "save us from the Bolshevist terror." We found it difficult to appreciate their solicitude.

Our particular column of prisoners was more fortunate than many others. We numbered only seven hundred, but we were reasonably equipped, were directed by a competent and fairly conscientious German staff and were just generally lucky.

Many prisoners from other camps fared badly. Some of those from Wehrmacht camps for enlisted men, poorly nourished for years, fell sick en route and were left behind along the snow-choked highways. Some were never heard from again.

It was hard going. We were not used to protracted physical effort of this kind. The snow made walking difficult. The sleds became heavier as the hours passed. Many prisoners began to lighten their loads; we could not afford to carry superfluous baggage. I had brought with me a treasured German beer stein, a beautiful piece with a delicately worked silver top. It was my one souvenir of my prison years. I tossed it into the ditch. The ditch was soon strewn with violins and guitars, books, trumpets, framed family pictures — precious items in a prisoner's "life savings."

We were on the road for a week.

At night our column was herded into farmyards, where we were left to shift for ourselves. Some of us bedded in haylofts; others, with the cattle in the warmer mangers or in abandoned chicken coops and wine cellars. Each night found us cold and footsore, but morale was still high and there was always occasion for a laugh.

The first night found us billetted in a huge barn that was half-filled with hay. The Germans had ordered all seven hundred of us into the barn and had then set up guard posts outside. The doors had been closed, and we were told that no exit would be permitted under any circumstances and that it was "*rauchen verboten!*"

"No smoking! They must be crazy. Who'd

dream of lighting up in here? This hay is tinder dry."

We had no trouble keeping warm. We were packed in so tightly that one man's feet were in another's face. It took some time before each man had settled himself in some kind of comfort for the night. Many of us had removed our boots and filled them with crunched-up newspaper to dry them out while we slept.

We learned other tricks.

"Hey, fellas . . ." It was one of the Yanks, the boy from the Ozarks who had been a crop-duster pilot before he switched to RAF Hurricanes. "Take off your socks and stick them under your armpits. They'll be all nice and cosy when you put them on in the morning."

The barn lacked any kind of latrine.

"There's only one thing for it, boys. Anyone wants to pee will have to get up against the barn wall and let it go against the boards. Okay?"

Sleep was fitful. Throughout the night I kept waking to the sound of stumbling feet making their way through sleeping bodies, the sound of cursing and then the splashing against the barn boards.

And then that one never-to-be-forgotten moment when a one-liner, uttered in the most impeccable Oxford accent, almost lifted the barn roof with the laughter of seven hundred men: "Jesus Christ, old boy, that was my face!"

There were many things about that winter march that will never be forgotten. One was the kindness of German women in the villages through which we passed. Time and time again, as the guards herded our ragged line along wintry streets, women and girls came out into the road with jugs and buckets of water. Sometimes it was hot water, sometimes even a mug of milk. They knew who and what we were, knew we were the enemy; yet somehow they felt it was more important to see us merely as men in distress and to give what comfort they could.

One bitterly poignant scene stands out above the others. In one of the villages a pretty German girl of teen age came to the street curb with a jug of hot water. A particularly unpleasant guard, sticking rigidly to the order not to permit any civilian contact with the prisoners, knocked the jug from her hand. We plodded by silently through the dirty snow while the girl stood there, with empty hands held out to us in a hopeless gesture, tears rolling down her cheeks.

The attitude of the guarding Germans fluctuated between this inflexible adherence to orders and a sometimes fatherly interest in our physical welfare.

During one of the periodic rest breaks the new prisoners among us, those who had not yet had time to acquire a smattering of German, sounded a loud and indignant protest when the German major in charge of the column began to shout at several prisoners who were sitting down in the snow to rest their legs.

"Bloody Prussian bastard! Won't even let a man sit down to rest. That's a German for you! Dirty son of a bitch!"

Others among us laughed. The major's parade-ground screaming had merely expressed his concern that by sitting on the cold ground his wards might contract *Hämorrhoiden!*

Perhaps the most memorable interlude in the week's march came with the two days we spent bivouacked on a big rambling farm estate near the village of Gross Selten. It was a welcome break in the wintry trek westward and brought fresh excitement in the form of new company. The houses and other living quarters in the complex were filled with civilian refugees, women and children from the bombed-out cities of the Ruhr and the Rhine. And in the haylofts and cattle stalls that became our quarters we found ourselves bedmates with the 235 survivors of the elite SS Hermann Göring Division, retreating after three disastrous and bloody engagements with the Russians.

While the rest of our column was scattered in the cattle stalls and haylofts, about six of us had discovered a shelter in a root cellar under one of the barns. There was only a skimpy layer of straw between our weary bodies and the winter store of potatoes and turnips, but the place was warm. We had found some candles somewhere around the village, purchased out of our stock of cigarettes, and while our cellar was an eerie cave of shadows, we thought ourselves luckier than most.

We were barely awake the next morning when a woman came down the stone steps with a basket on her arm. She gestured to us sharply to get up and give her access to the vegetables. She watched

us with a frown as we scrambled out of her way,
and we saw that she hadn't missed the air force insignia still visible on our frayed and dirty tunics.

"Air gangsters," she muttered.

As she gathered the vegetables into her basket,
she punctuated her effort with the bitter invective
borrowed from the German press and radio. At one
point she straightened up to point an accusing
finger at a pilot's badge.

"Terror bomber!"

She scraped around under the straw for a few
more turnips and then started back towards the
stone stairs. She turned on the first step to confront
us once more.

"Baby killers!"

After the woman left, we crawled up into the
daylight. The sun was shining, but it was icy cold.
In the centre of the big farm courtyard a motley
mob of POWs and SS troopers were warming themselves around a gasoline-fired blast heater. It had
been used on the Russian front to thaw out frozen
tanks. Now there were no tanks left, and no guns,
so the heater was being used strictly for humans.

We washed and shaved at the trough in the
middle of the courtyard. It was a magnificent horse
trough, fashioned from an enormous slab of silvery
granite. The water had frozen during the night, but
earlier shavers had already broken the ice. For
us, shaving was not only a matter of morale and
personal pride; it was also a matter of German
regulations. Officer prisoners were expected to be
clean-shaven at all times.

The Germans were also shaving at the trough,

cursing the bits of broken ice. I caught a sense that we were trying to impress each other with our Spartan hardiness and military élan. We found ourselves looking at each other with curiosity, and not without a certain respect. The SS badge may have become an object of opprobrium elsewhere in the world, but these men were not of the *Polizie-SS*, Hitler's barbaric execution squads, but were the *Waffen-SS*, Germany's equivalent of our guards regiments — tough, disciplined soldiers who in one battle after another had made the Russians earn their victories.

We were not ashamed to be shaving in the same horse trough with them. In fact, although we had only met up with them the day before, we were fast becoming buddies. It was a simple matter of economics.

Our food supply was exhausted. The cold and the effort of trudging through slush and snow had imposed unforeseen demands on our Red Cross parcels. But there was food in the SS trucks. The *Hermann Göring* boys had sensibly hung on to their supply of beef-and-hardtack biscuits, and their trucks were full. But they were short of cigarettes, of which we still had a plentiful supply. On leaving the camp we had stuffed our shirts, jackets and even our boots with cigarettes. In the chaos of a collapsing Third Reich, cigarettes had become hard currency. It was a perfect situation for barter. We swapped cigarettes for hardtack with the SS men, to our mutual comfort and good cheer.

Shaved and shivering, I sidled up to the gang basking in the tropical hurricane from the blast

heater and casually produced a pack of Lucky
Strikes. Two or three of the SS took a fag from the
pack. But when one of them reached out for a
cigarette, his hand was smacked aside by the
trooper next to him.

"He's too young to smoke!"

Several of us began to laugh. We found it incredible that this soldier, who had braved months
of the cruel and bloody eastern front and survived,
was yet too young to smoke. But the SS men didn't
share our laughter. Orders were orders. *Befehl ist
Befehl.* They had a duty to protect their young
comrade from bad habits.

A little later, poking about the ancient farm
complex, we came across three of the SS trying to
free the runners of an old sled from the block of ice
in which they were embedded. They laughingly
pointed to the nearby highway sloping down a long
hill to a crossroads village in the valley below. The
farmer's old cutter, with the shafts removed, would
make a toboggan, and they planned to enjoy some
coasting.

We helped them break the cutter out of the ice.
What ensued during the next few hours was something I didn't talk about for many years after the
war's end. Upon our return home, the only thing
people wanted to hear were tales of heroism,
atrocities and the tribulations of brave men. How
could I have told them about a wonderful day in the
midst of the Death March, with the Russian guns
hammering less than thirty miles away, when
some Allied aircrew joined a coasting party with
members of the *Waffen-SS?*

It was the finest kind of fun, and the day was made for it. The snow sparkled under a blinding winter sun, and the highway was a tobogganist's glacial dream. We shouted and we screamed as we raced down the slope and careened into the ditch and then, laughing and panting, laboriously pushed and pulled the ancient sled back up the hill again.

For us it was a wild and intoxicating break from the long years behind the barbed wire. For the SS men I sensed it was a relief from the tensions and horrors of the *Ostfront.* For both groups it was a few priceless hours of just being boys again.

At morning's end we were exhausted. We made another cigarettes-for-hardtack swap with the SS boys; then crept back into our root cellar to chew on the dry biscuits and rest.

We had just settled ourselves down on the straw when the refugee woman paid us another call. She came with a galvanized bucket, wreathed in steam. The bucket was filled with a thick, hot vegetable stew. She set the bucket down on the floor in front of us and gave us a strange, twisted smile.

"Baby killers," she said and then turned and vanished up the steps.

It was a wondrous day at Gross Selten.

XIV

This Terrible Swift Sword

The last leg of that winter migration, after the week on the open road, was by train. Our footslogging ended at the town of Spremberg, and after a scanty meal given us in a Wehrmacht transport garage we were marched to the railroad station and entrained. We learned that our destination was a camp near the town of Luckenwalde, about twenty miles south of Berlin on the main line between Berlin and Leipzig.

This time we had far from first-class transportation. We were bundled into ordinary boxcars and the doors locked behind us. There were no windows of any kind, and the only light was what filtered weakly through the cracks between the wooden boards. A single wooden box had been placed in the middle of the car to serve as our latrine. So many of us had been packed into each car that there was not room for everyone to stretch out and rest at the same time.

We were dismayed and apprehensive.

The long trek through the winter countryside may have been physically trying, but we had at least been in the open, moving through new landscapes and seeing new faces. Even the presence of the guards hadn't dulled an excited sense of limited freedom. There had been so many contacts with the outside world, along with the overriding conviction that each hour brought us closer to ultimate liberty somewhere down the road.

Now that feeling was gone.

The big sliding doors of the boxcar had no sooner shut than gloom settled over the company.

"Jesus . . . we're on the main line to Berlin. The way the Yanks are hitting this area now we'll never make it. They're over here every day, fighters and bombers, shooting up everything that moves. We're sitting ducks!"

It wasn't a pleasant prospect.

"Yeah, with the Russians on the Oder and the Allies on the Rhine, we're about the only targets left to shoot up. Going to Berlin by train is like playing Russian roulette!"

But there still could be laughter.

"Yeah, there's so little of Germany left their fighters have to keep banking just to stay over their own territory!"

And the incurable card players were still with us. Their first complaint was that there was not enough light to see the cards. One of their number soon fixed that. It took an hour of patient labour, but with his pocket knife he was able to enlarge a crack between the boards to a full three-quarters of an inch. With that much light, as long as the players stayed close to it, the game could go on.

Night brought an ebbing of morale. Sleep was impossible. There was a continuous and painful struggle to find some way of meshing an assortment of restless arms, legs and necks in some pattern compatible with even the most minimal degree of comfort. The odour of sweat from half a hundred unwashed bodies mingled with the stench from the "thunderbox." There were frequent halts at sidings along the route, and in the dark silence we could hear the ominous, throbbing drone of Bomber Command squadrons moving in on their targets.

All of us were keyed up in the tension compounded of claustrophobia, fear and fatigue, and when one of us suddenly broke under the strain there was no sense of disesteem.

"I want my mother . . . I want my mother."

The words came sobbing out of the darkness. We all knew who it was. The voice was that of a young fighter pilot whom we knew had at least three enemy kills to his credit and who had been shot down over the French coast in 1942. He was a bright, dynamic personality and in camp had been consistently cheerful and co-operative.

"I want my mother . . ."

There was some scuffling in the darkness; someone was wrestling his way through the tangle of arms, legs and torsos.

"Okay, boy . . . it's all right now. We'll get you to your mother. It's all right. . . . There now, get some rest."

Wally Floody had the distraught man in his arms and was rocking him gently, as he would a baby. The sobbing slowly subsided. A personal crisis had come and gone.

In all the years of Stalag Luft 3 no one prisoner had earned more respect than Flight Lieutenant Wally Floody. But the admiration we all had for Wally reached its zenith that night in the boxcar when he played the role of mother.

The lower one's morale, the less it takes to restore it. It was cold, with a drizzling rain, when the train disgorged us into the railway yard at Luckenwalde the following evening. Once we were out of the boxcar's stench, had planted our feet on the cindery ground and taken a breath of cold, damp, refreshing air, our flagging spirits revived.

The Germans marched us out of the railway yards, past the station and into one of the town's main streets. Somebody started to sing *Pack Up Your Troubles in Your Old Kit Bag*, and within a few minutes the whole column was belting out *It's a Long, Long Way to Tipperary*. The guards made no sign that they objected to our singing. We had the distinct impression that they were much more dejected than even we had been while on the train.

The singing brought many of the townsfolk into the street. They stood in doorways and watched in silence as we marched past. Painfully conscious of the miserable spectacle we presented, we made an effort to look "undaunted and unbowed," or at least as if we were soldiers.

We had just come to the end of one of the songs when a second-storey window of one of the houses flew open and a woman thrust out her head.

"Hey! Hey! I say, you chaps, did any of you ever read Jerome K. Jerome's *Three Men in a Boat?*"

A number of prisoners at once shouted back their affirmation.

"Jolly fine book, wasn't it?" she called.

Before anyone could reply to that, her head had vanished and the window had slammed shut. We tramped on in mystified silence. It was one more bizarre bit of absurdity encapsulated in the larger absurdity of war.

It was dark by the time we reached the camp, which seemed to be a mile or two beyond the town limits. The Germans had decided that we must all go through a hot shower before being admitted to the barrack blocks. We were lined up in front of the shower block, waiting in the rain while one small group after another was permitted in. There was an anteroom just inside the door where one disrobed, piling one's clothes on a bench or in a heap on the floor. The showers were beyond, through an open door.

The shower room was brightly lighted, but the light was mistily diffused by the steamy vapour so that the figures twisting and turning under the showers were only hazily seen. I had almost finished undressing when a voice beside me made me look closer into the shower room.

"Jesus — there are women in there!"

I couldn't believe what I saw. I squinted to make sure. I could see two, three, then four and five nude bodies glistening in the hazy light. Or as much of the bodies as we could see. Most of their bodies, from the head down to below the waist, was obscured by long, ebony-black strands of hair.

"Such long hair," somebody said in the hush.

But the sense of shock and embarrassment was short-lived. One of the British prisoners, who had rudely poked his head a little farther into the shower room, suddenly laughed.

"You idiots! They're not women — they're Sikhs. Captured in North Africa. It's against their religion to cut their hair. Come on, you guys, let's get a shower!"

It was a suitable introduction to life in Stalag 3A, which, along with Stalag 8B at Lamsdorf, was perhaps one of the worst Wehrmacht prison camps in Germany.

Stalag 3A was reputed to be the worst prison camp in Germany. It had been used as a punishment camp, especially for French, Russian and Polish prisoners used as slave labour in German industry. Guards at the slave-labour barracks scattered through Germany had been issued with German-French language phrase books, in which could be found the warning:

"If you don't behave I'll have you sent to Luckenwalde!"

Perhaps the statement that the camp's mass-grave cemetery held 15,000 corpses, half the current population of the camp, will afford the best idea of what the Luckenwalde camp was like.

At Stalag 3A we slept two hundred men to a room, packed in three-tiered shelves like cordwood, and kept warm solely by pure animal heat and the dirty sacking stuffed with wood shavings into which we crept for comfort. There were no Red Cross parcels at Stalag 3A, no recreational facilities of any kind and, apart from the introductory shower upon arrival, rarely enough water in which to wash.

Ironically, the one and only piece of reading material in our own entire compound — and no one had the slightest idea of where it had come from — was a coverless, dog-eared copy of Milton's *Areopagitica*, his lordly treatise on freedom of the press. I have no idea of how well that book has fared on the bookshelves of the world; in Stalag 3A it was permanently on the best-seller list.

But if the pervading atmosphere was gloomy and depressing, there were compensating highlights. One was the presence in our compound of the Poles. We had about forty Polish officers with us, all army men who had been in captivity since the first weeks of the war. They were uniformly splendid, enduring types of men who quickly won our admiration. I came to know some of them well, after it had been suggested that I should pass the

time teaching English to those who wished to learn
the language.

It was an interesting exercise. Since most of the
Poles spoke excellent German, and mine was only a
shattered parody of the tongue in which I had to
give instruction, my efforts probably amounted
more to entertainment than education. But we
made some progress, and in the process I found
some engaging friends.

There was Alfred Zimmerman, a slight,
dynamic Jew who had been married only a short
time before he was taken prisoner in 1939. He had
heard nothing from or about his wife since, and
while he feared the worst he was always hoping
that war's end might find her for him.

Zimmerman had been conscripted into the
Polish army; he had little use for the military life.
He had been born and brought up in the vicinity of
Kolomyja, in the Carpathian foothills, and had
some terrifying memories from childhood days of
the bitter World War I struggle between Russians
and Austrians.

"They fought all through the village once, and
the next day they gathered up the dead and laid out
the bodies in the schoolyard, all in nice neat rows,"
he said.

"The bodies were all face up — perhaps a hundred of them. There was no school that day, but we
kids couldn't keep away from the place — we found
it terribly fascinating. We played a game with the
bodies. We went up and down the rows and lifted
the eyelids of the dead men. It was a guessing game

we played. Blue eyes or brown eyes? Blue eyes . . .
brown eyes."

Zimmerman had other interesting bits of information. The Scots were not the only people to play
the bagpipes, he said. Why, the Polish folks up in
the hills around Kolomyja had been playing the
pipes for years. He thought that perhaps that is
where the pipes originated. After all, he said, the
Celts had passed through Eastern Europe on their
way to the British Isles, perhaps dropping off
bagpipes on the way.

Our Poles had another contribution to make —
they could sing. Their voices were magnificent,
often with the spine-tingling timbre of the opera
house. Never before or since have I heard the
human voice so gloriously triumphant, so spon-
taneously joyous, as I did on Easter Sunday of 1945
in Stalag 3A. A priest had turned up from somewhere among the sprawling compounds, and the
Poles had arranged to participate in a High Mass.

They had constructed an altar of old bits of
lumber and wooden boxes, and draped it with a
clean white sheet. The altar was placed in a sandy
spot between two barrack blocks so that the
prisoners attending might be sheltered from the
raw east wind. The choir of Polish voices, strong
and vibrant, made it one of the most stirring
musical performances I have ever attended. As
they sang, the wretchedness of our surroundings
faded into insignificance, and we felt ourselves
kindled anew with the vanquishing Spirit of Man.

Something else was steadily overshadowing

our physical miseries. We had the noise of history in a great crescendo all around us. The last great offensive was under way before the snows had gone. The Russians were across the Oder, and in the west the British and Americans were over the Rhine.

But the approach of the enemy prompted the Germans to attempt once more to move us. It was announced that the British and American officers were to be moved south, with the implication that we would be held in Hitler's rumoured "Bavarian Redoubt" as hostages in the event of certain nebulous negotiations of which the German hierarchy was still dreaming.

And so it was back to the Luckenwalde railway yards again, where a row of boxcars on a siding was to be our home for the next four or five days. We would have to wait there, we were told, until the authorities could find a locomotive to haul the train south.

We weren't happy with the decision and made every effort to delay our evacuation from the camp. All the news gave promise of an early appearance of the Allies, and we didn't relish the prospect of being held hostage by last-ditch Nazi fanatics in the mountains of Bavaria during the dying agonies of the Third Reich.

Our redoubtable Dr. Monteuis did his best to stop the move. We had just finished one distressing migration, he told the Germans, and were in no condition to face another. Most of us, he assured them, were little better than cripples. The Germans ignored him, but as we were being lined up in preparation for the march to the railway yards Dr.

Monteuis appeared, and with some grotesque and exaggerated pantomime encouraged us to simulate the condition he had described.

We hobbled out of the main gate like a congregation of sick and tired old men from a senior citizens' home.

As it turned out, the sojourn in the railway yard was, by contrast to life in the Stalag, something of a holiday. In the face of the deteriorating military situation, German discipline was visibly weakening. The boxcars were for sleeping only; during the day we were free to roam at will through the railway yards. Limits were set by the presence of sentries and machine-gun posts at various points around the perimeter.

Very few trains were running.

About mid-afternoon one day, a still smartly turned-out passenger train pulled in from the direction of Berlin. It was obviously headed south for the last remaining piece of Germany not immediately threatened by the shrinking fronts.

I was suddenly reminded of the Rome-Berlin Express, which I had seen passing through Leipzig almost three years before. Although much had changed since then, this train seemed a duplicate of that other. There was a dining car, and the passengers we could see through the windows seemed to be dining just as if it were peacetime again. They had the same immaculate napery, the same sparkling glassware, the same deferential waiters.

There was one difference.

Attached to this train were two flak cars, heavily armoured cars bristling with antiaircraft guns.

There was one at the rear of the train and another just behind the locomotive.

I have often wondered if those passengers survived. Shortly after the train had steamed out of the station, an entire squadron of P-47 Thunderbolts loomed out of the western sky a few miles to the south of us. We watched as one after another they peeled off and dropped earthward in a screaming dive. They were completely unopposed; there were no German fighters to be seen.

We could hear bombs bursting and a little later the thundering of the P-47 cannonfire as the aircraft rose and dived repeatedly in attacks on whatever may have been in their gunsights. The next town south of Luckenwalde was Jüterbog, an important railway junction, and was almost certain to have been the target. It was just about as certain that the passenger train was in the same area, and would almost certainly have come under attack.

I felt sorry for whoever may have been on that train. But I was even happier that the train had been there to draw the fire and that the P-47s had chosen Jüterbog for their target instead of the railway yards of Luckenwalde.

There was something else to make me happy that day. In our comparative freedom we had been able to stroll along the high wire fence that separated the railway yard from one of the town streets. Schools were still functioning, and we enjoyed watching the children marching back and forth to school. On this occasion school was just out, and several of us found ourselves looking through the wire at half a dozen nicely dressed children who were eyeing us with great curiosity.

One of them, a girl of about ten or twelve, spoke to us. Her English was close to perfect.

"Would you like us to sing English?"

It was a magical moment. It seemed quite unreal. It was so unreal, under the circumstances, that the girl might just as easily have been Little Red Riding Hood or Goldilocks.

"Please, we'd love to hear you sing English."

She turned to the others, and they conferred for a moment in giggling German. Then they lined up shoulder to shoulder, opened their mouths and sang:

> Baa! Baa! Black sheep, have you any wool?
> Yes, sir, yes, sir! Three bags full,
> One for my master, and one for my dame,
> But none for the naughty boy that cries in
>   the lane.

For the remaining few days of our stay in the railway yards, we made a point of intercepting our small friends on their way home from school and were each time refreshed with *Baa! Baa! Black Sheep.*

The song became one more of my most precious memories of wartime Germany.

We lost track of time, but it must have been on the fourth or fifth day in the railway yards that the Germans realized there were no more locomotives available. In any event, as one of them confided to us, the almost daily air raids had rendered most of the lines to the south impassable. We were lined up once more and marched back to the squalor of Stalag 3A.

Squalid as it was, Luckenwalde gave us a grandstand seat for the final contest of the war, the Battle of Berlin. Vast armadas of Allied bombers, escorted by weaving swarms of long-range fighters, droned daily in tight formations across the camp on their way to the German capital and industrial targets beyond. By night the sky came to be almost permanently lighted by nervously fingering searchlights, by the red, green and yellow target indicators, by the staccato flicker of the photoflashes, and by the ominous orange glow of burning buildings.

Luckenwalde also brought us one last and perhaps sentimental link with Hermann Göring, the *Reichsmarschall* and commander of the Luftwaffe. His was the face that had confronted me on waking that first morning of captivity three years earlier. He had played host at dinner in the Hotel Bristol in Berlin to the first air force prisoner of war, Squadron Leader Wank Murray. And our Christmas beer had come with the compliments of Hermann Göring.

So it seemed only fitting that one of the very last aircrew prisoners to arrive in camp should also have been touched by Hermann Göring. He was Captain Monroe Hotaling, of the U.S. Army Air Corps, who was shot down in his Flying Fortress B-17 during a daylight raid on Oranienburg, just north of Berlin. He had landed in his parachute in the grounds of Karinhall, Göring's magnificent estate, and had quickly been picked up by several of the estate guards.

The guards had taken him to the huge mansion, and within a few minutes Hotaling found himself standing in front of the *Reichsmarschall.*

"I knew who it was at once," Hotaling told us. "He seemed delighted when he saw I had recognized him, and was in great humour. He had been having some kind of conference with a bunch of generals, but he seemed much more interested in my company than theirs. And he invited me to have dinner with him."

It was a typical Göring repast. The great man had been in the process of killing off some of his estate animals. The meal included venison and buffalo meat, with roast goose, some fine wine, and brandy and Havana cigars to finish.

"He said he had been impressed by the American daylight operations — talked about discipline and integrity of our crews and all that. He confessed that his Luftwaffe had been unable to turn us back."

Hotaling spent the night at Karinhall. The next morning the *Reichsmarschall* sent him off to prison camp literally in state — he travelled in a beautiful carriage drawn by a team of coal-black stallions, which, Göring told him proudly, were a gift from Marshal Mannerheim of Finland. The carriage had taken him only partway to Luckenwalde. He had finished the journey in a Wehrmacht truck.

"Guess they couldn't take a chance on letting those horses get all the way to Luckenwalde," one of the boys joked. "Here they would have been eaten!"

Hotaling, along with the rest of us, was able to witness from the ground and at close range the last and perhaps the most spectacular mass daylight raid of the war in Europe. It was the great raid on Berlin just a few days before the Russians loosed their final offensive against the capital.

The day had dawned without a cloud in the sky. The first wave of bombers appeared shortly before noon, flying at about 25,000 feet. Their vapour trails left a lacy network of white ribbons across the blue sky. Escorting fighters weaved back and forth across the track of the bombers. As succeeding waves of bombers appeared, the sky soon became completely overcast. The bombers seemed to be coming from every direction. There were Fortresses and RAF heavies from Britain and more Fortresses and Liberators from bases in Italy. That day we counted no less than 2,200 aircraft — bombers and fighters — over Berlin. Their contrails blotted out the sun.

We could feel the shock waves in the ground under our feet, but as the bombing progressed and the shocks intensified the very sky above us began to tremble. The vapour trails had melded into a silvery film, and the concussion from the bomb blasts sent enormous concentric rings radiating out across the sky from the target area, much like the rings made when a stone is dropped into a pool of water.

It was something none of us had ever seen before, and likely would never see again. There was something frightening and apocalyptic about it; it seemed the epitome of doom. Both heaven and earth were trembling in concert, in compulsive protest against such unparalleled violence. As we stood watching and listening, our emotions were a nervous mix of humility and awe.

As I watched and wondered, a line kept running through my head:

> *He is trampling out the vintage*
> *Where the grapes of wrath are stored.*

And I knew for certain that "this terrible swift sword" was the promise of liberation.

XV

Liberation

It was the night before Adolf Hitler's birthday, and the German doctor attached to the camp, a big, portly, good-natured fellow who had welcomed the arrival of our Dr. Monteuis, came breathlessly into the barrack block to break the news.

"They're coming in this direction — they're on the way. Our lines have broken around Kottbus and the Russians are pouring through!"

There was no official confirmation, either from

the radio communiqués of the *Oberkommando der Wehrmacht* or those from our concealed radio link with the BBC. But we had all the confirmation we needed. Kottbus itself was about fifty miles southeast of the camp, but we could see clearly the reflection from great fires in the night sky and hear the muffled rumble of artillery.

The next morning was April 20. The rumbling to the east and southeast continued, and around mid-morning another great air raid was under way over Berlin.

"Happy birthday, dear Adolf, happy birthday to you!" The rude greeting was heard over and over again whenever a particularly shattering bomb blast shook what windows remained in the barrack blocks.

A little later it was confirmed that the Russians had penetrated as far as Dahme, about twenty miles distant, and were pounding German defensive positions around the railway junction of Jüterbog, just ten miles to the south.

It was around noon, too, that we noticed some of the Germans drifting away from the *Kommandantur* area. Our friend Paul, who had tramped all the way from Sagan with us, sought me out in the dingy corner of the barrack where I bunked. I felt sorry for him. His face was drawn and tired. I tried to imagine what it must be like for a proud German in this hour of such crushing defeat and chaos.

"I'll be going soon," he said. "It's all over. I don't know what's going to happen — the wife and kids are still in Magdeburg. Maybe the Americans will get there first. Anyway, I'm going to try to make it through the lines."

He hesitated for a moment and then drew from his tunic pocket a fountain pen and a square of cardboard about the size of a postcard. He looked at me in embarrassment.

"You could help me . . . I don't know what I might run up against . . . I tried to do the right thing by the prisoners, you know that . . . *vielleicht*, perhaps you could write a good word for me?"

For the question in his eyes there was only one answer. I took the card and wrote. It was something to the effect that Paul Reemt-Heeren was a good German soldier who had done the best he could to make life more comfortable for the prisoners in his charge. I signed it with my name, rank and serial number, and my Canadian address.

He thanked me. We shook hands. He touched his cap in a friendly salute and went his way. Months later I was to hear from him. He had succeeded in slipping through the lines and had found his wife and children alive and well with the Americans in Magdeburg. It made me happy. Paul was yet another good memory of my German years.

The "birthday party" became more exciting that evening. There was more than a glow in the sky in the direction of the Russian front. At times we could actually see flames leaping above the skyline, and the ephemeral glow of tracer fire. By the following morning it was clear that the end was near. About dawn we were awakened by an ear-

splitting roar of artillery. The Russians had obviously spent the night moving the guns to positions within a few miles of us, and they were now
pouring their prodigious fire into the town of
Luckenwalde itself.

It was as if the end of the world had come.

Hour after hour the awful barrage continued.
There was never a pause for even a few seconds.
We could see bricks, stones, steel girders and pieces
of timber flying high into the sky as one direct hit
followed another. As on the day of the great bombing raid on Berlin, there was no sun that day. It had
been blotted out almost as soon as it had risen by
an enormous mushrooming ball of smoke.

The Germans quit the camp shortly after noon.
A runner brought a message to the senior guard on
duty at the main gate into the compound. The
guard heard the message and looked in at the little
group of prisoners standing expectantly behind the
barbed wire. Then he unhooked the keys from his
belt, flashed us a big grin, tossed the keys over the
barbed wire of the gate and shuffled away.

At the same time another messenger arrived
from the *Kommandantur*, seeking the senior Allied
officer. The *Kommandant*, a Colonel Lutter, wished
to confer with him. Our senior Allied officer at that
time was General Otto Ruge, a Norwegian. He was
busy at a more important conference within the
camp and sent his second-in-command, Lieutenant
Colonel Walter Oakes, an American airman out of
Texas.

The *Kommandant* met Oakes outside the door
to the administrative offices. He told Oakes that he

and the German security force were evacuating the camp. He asked for assurance that the prisoners would remain within the camp and would offer no hindrance to the German defence of the Luckenwalde area.

Oakes gave him the assurance he asked for. All the prisoners, he said, were now under the command of General Ruge, and for their own safety it had been decided that they should remain in the compounds.

While he was speaking, a large group of prisoners, all wearing white armbands and marching in military formation, emerged from the compound into the *Kommandantur*. Colonel Lutter looked at them in astonishment.

"How can you tell me nobody will leave the camp? Who and what are those men doing?"

Oakes told him. "They are our provost marshal's guard, our police. Your guards are leaving — our men will now take over the guarding of the camp!"

The Germans left.

All that day and evening the Russian barrage continued. About ten o'clock it stopped as suddenly as it had begun. For the remainder of the night we were engulfed in the silence of the dead. Not a single rifle shot broke the terrible stillness. Nobody slept. The tension was almost more than one could bear. All of us waited for the dawn.

Dawn came that day, April 22, at 6:15 a.m. At that moment a tiny, two-manned armoured car, no bigger than a jeep, braked to a halt outside the main gate. An unkempt, hatless man with a tommy-gun in his hand stood in the turret. He brandished the gun and shouted at us to open the gate.

The moment he opened his mouth to speak, we knew this was the moment we had been waiting for. We knew we were free. A great shout went up from a hundred throats. The man was speaking Russian. Here, after all these years, was a man with a gun, and he wasn't a German!

In the half-hour that followed, men behaved as they had never behaved before. As the little armoured car crept slowly through the streets of the camp, the whole population of Stalag 3A went crazy. Time and again the vehicle came to a stop in a solid mass of laughing, yelling and crying humanity.

I saw men patting and stroking the steel plates of the armoured car as if it were some beloved animal. Men kissed the cold metal, affectionately pinched the tires. All around, prisoners were hugging one another and dancing in crazy abandon. Everyone was laughing, or crying, or doing both at once, without even realizing it.

The demonstration reached its crazy zenith when the armoured car found itself entrapped in a solid phalanx of Russian prisoners. They were more physically demonstrative than we had been. They dragged the man with the tommy-gun from his turret and commenced to toss him into the air, catching him as he came down, kissing and hugging him and tossing him skywards again. Only when he lost his temper and began to scream invectives at them did they let him back into his turret.

A few hours later the mad, delirious performance was repeated when the armoured spearhead
of the regiment that had taken Luckenwalde rolled
victoriously into the camp, the great tanks
smashing down the hated barbed-wire fences as
they rolled along. It was the Third Guards Tank
Regiment of the First Ukrainian Front.

Thrill followed thrill.

The first women some of us had seen in years
were riding on the T-34s and the big, grim Stalin
tanks. Tommy-guns rested in their laps, and
sometimes big revolvers were thrust holsterless
through their belts. Some wore bandages covering
their wounds from the day before. Side by side with
the men, they had fought their way through some
of the fiercest actions of World War II. A few hours
later they would be rolling into Potsdam for the
final assault on Hitler's empire.

That was our day, our day of liberation.

XVI

Celebrations

The Russians had arrived just in time. With the steadily shrinking frontiers of the German Reich and the round-the-clock bombing of roads and railways, the Red Cross parcels that had become a trickle in February ceased coming altogether in March and April. Then the standard daily German ration of barley, potatoes and bread shrank to the vanishing point, and a thin, hideous concoction we called grass soup was substituted.

In fact, we were down to our last ounce of caviar the day the Russians came. Bizarre as it may sound, caviar had been our only solid food for about two weeks. Conditions in the camp had become so bad that a plea had gone out to the Swedish Red Cross for immediate emergency aid. Through the energetic interest of Count Folke Bernadotte, we were told, food was on the way. When it arrived, it turned out to be three railway boxcars filled with caviar!

The caviar, which came in gallon-sized square tins, was the finest kind of protein and stood us in good stead. It was also very salty. For several days we could relish it, especially since the grass soup had been entirely without salt for a few weeks. Luckenwalde had even run out of salt. But during the last few days of the caviar diet, the thirst level of the camp had reached a painful peak.

The advent of the Russians put an end to the famine at Stalag 3A. The Russian officer who had taken command of the camp, Major Ledbedev, announced that we were to have access to a major Wehrmacht food depot, which the Russians had seized during their advance. It was at Fort Zinna, site of a huge Wehrmacht training centre about seven or eight miles distant. At Fort Zinna, he said, we would find all the food we needed.

He would supply the trucks for transport and armed guards for the operation, but he had no men to spare for loading and off-loading the cargoes. The prisoners would have to assume that chore.

It was a task we scrambled for. The prospect of riding in a truck, of moving freely through the conquered countryside, of muscular activity in so practical an application, was a prospect too good to miss. We looked upon the duty as an exciting excursion.

Will Higgins and I were fortunate enough to be drafted on one of the first days of Fort Zinna duty. Each truck was manned by two prisoners, and the Russian driver was accompanied by a second Russian riding shotgun. Both carried with them the ubiquitous Red Army tommy-guns. Berlin had not yet fallen, and the German 9th Army, 12,000 strong, was still in the vicinity, fighting desperately to cut across the highway through Luckenwalde and drive to "sanctuary" with the Americans over the Elbe.

That first trip to Fort Zinna is yet another indelible memory from the liberation days. Higgins and I travelled in the body of the truck. Neither of the Russians in the cab had any German, so communication was limited to spasmodic grins and friendly gestures of the hands. The trip to Fort Zinna was sheer joy. I was standing in the rear of the truck, a red kerchief around my neck, the wind blowing my hair awry, feeling like a swashbuckling bandit. The wind had the smell of freedom.

Fort Zinna had been untouched by the fighting and had fallen into Russian hands intact. We passed through the main gate into a vast, sprawling complex of huge, white concrete warehouses. Our Russians knew exactly where to go, and in a few minutes we found ourselves backing up to the loading platform of one of the warehouses.

Just inside the door were some trolleys stacked

high with big cardboard cartons. One of the Russians indicated that these were what we were to load onto the truck. Each carton must have weighed thirty or forty pounds and was filled with margarine. Another truck was loading from an adjacent door along the ramp — bags of beans, judging from the spillage on the ramp.

As soon as our Russians showed us what had to be done, they disappeared. About a half-hour later Higgins and I had finished loading the margarine. The truck was piled high with cartons, leaving only a small squared-in place where we could sit for the ride home. We sat down on the edge of the loading platform and swung our legs, resting from the unaccustomed exercise.

We were alerted by an unusual sound — a discreet hissing noise.

"Psst! Psst!"

I couldn't tell where it came from. I looked around, but there was no one visible in the warehouse door.

"Hey, it's down there," said Higgins.

There was a small window at ground level, off to one side. It obviously served some kind of cellar or basement. I jumped down from the platform and ran to investigate.

One of the Russians was peering up at me. He had such a typically Slav face, round, flat and somehow ingenuously boyish. And it was wrinkled into a roguish grin. The Russian put his finger to his lips in a conspiratorial gesture, ducked back into the darkness and then reappeared to thrust something at me through the window.

It was a case of wine.

It was open at the top, and I could see that it was full. Twelve bottles. Red wine. My heart was dancing. If it had been a case of gold bricks, I think I would have been disappointed. But twelve bottles of real, genuine, civilized wine. Higgins was right behind me, and his eyes were shining too.

We heaved the case up onto the truck and climbed up after it. In a few moments our two Russians appeared, checked to make sure we had the case of wine aboard and then climbed into the cab and started the engine.

About a mile down the highway, well away from the gates of Fort Zinna, the truck stopped. The Russians climbed out of the cab and came round to the rear. They signalled to us to let them have the case of wine. We watched with some puzzlement as one of the Russians took all the bottles out of the case and set them up, one next to the other, in a long line parallel to the curb of the pavement. The other Russian picked up the empty wooden case and hurled it into the bushes.

We were mystified.

Then the first Russian took a corkscrew from his pocket and methodically proceeded to pull the corks from all twelve bottles, tossing the corks aside as he did so.

I admired the straightforward way he worked. Having uncorked all the bottles, he straightened up, gave us a quick glance by way of taking census and then handed each one of us three opened bottles of wine. It seemed he did not intend them to be consumed at any great leisure.

And they weren't. We climbed back onto the truck, they returned to the cab and the journey resumed. I had taken a first few healthy swallows, but my first bottle was only half empty when the truck once again pulled over to the shoulder of the highway and stopped. The Russians emerged from the cab. Each carried one empty bottle.

About fifty feet away there was a low stone wall, greenish brown with moss. The Russians stood the two empties side by side on the wall. Then one of them returned to the truck to fetch his tommy-gun. He raised the gun and fired a burst, and the bottles flew high in little green pieces. The Russians roared with laughter and then turned to us and gestured for our bottles.

There was no escape. We had to gulp down what was left and hand them the bottles. This time it was the other Russian's turn to demolish the bottles, and then we climbed back on the truck and proceeded on our way. We guessed correctly that the next stop was not far off, and this time had conveniently emptied our bottles to match the capacity of our hosts. There was more fire from the tommy-gun and more hilarious laughter.

We had scarcely started on our third bottle when the truck came to a sudden halt. Straight ahead of us was an underpass, where the highway dipped under a railway line. The Russians parked the truck carefully on the shoulder of the road and then descended from the cab. This time they had no bottles with them, only the tommy-gun.

They walked the few yards down the road to

where it sloped under the bridge. I saw one of them point to the smooth, whitish grey concrete abutment supporting the superstructure. The Russians were laughing. They walked to the far side of the pavement, under the bridge, and then turned to face the opposite abutment, which was fifty or sixty feet distant.

There was a burst of fire, and then several more bursts.

These were followed by some good-natured bantering but derisive laughter from the other Russian, who grabbed the gun and did some firing of his own. We approached a little closer to see what kind of target they had, and it all suddenly became clear.

We weren't familiar with the Cyrillic alphabet used by the Russians, but we had seen the heiroglyphs before. Our Russians were using the tommy-gun to carve their initials on the concrete wall. The effort wasn't that expert, but the Russians seemed quite happy with their stab at immortality. They returned to the truck, parked the gun in the cab and then joined us in finishing off the wine. We thought them fine fellows when they pitched in to give us some much-needed help unloading the margarine back at Stalag 3A.

The Russian prisoners in Stalag 3A, who had been strictly segregated from all other nationalities, had quickly disappeared after the arrival of the Red Army. Many of them accepted the invitation to grab a rifle or a tommy-gun, board a truck and join in the impending onslaught on Berlin. Once the camp was liberated, we were free to enter the Russian compound, and what we found there astounded us.

The Russians had actually built a church in their compound. We couldn't believe our eyes. In our own compounds, even those in the holiday-camp environment of Stalag Luft 3, space would have been considered too precious if we had even had a mind to build a church, which none of us did. At Sagan we had enjoyed the luxury of a chaplain, the charming oblate priest who had been taken prisoner by a surface raider in the South Atlantic while he was en route to an African mission field. But we could not afford him more than a cramped cubbyhole for his glebe.

By contrast, the Russian compound at Stalag 3A had been deplorably overcrowded. The conditions we found in the barracks were indescribable. Nevertheless, the Russians had set aside one entire barrack block as a place of worship. Within a few days of our liberation, word of the Russian "cathedral" had spread far and wide, and we lost no time in making our pilgrimage.

We stood breathless upon opening the door.

A golden crucifix flashed from the altar, its radiance reflected in the prismed chandeliers that were suspended for the whole length of the nave. The windows were a splendour of stained glass, and along the walls were the Stations of the Cross, fashioned in brightly coloured mosaic. It was an incredible sight. We found it hard to understand how starved, beaten and often dying men could have found the inspiration and the energy to create so magnificent a place of worship.

When we looked a little closer, part of the miracle was explained. The golden crucifix was two pieces of two-by-four, painstakingly sheathed in gold-foil paper that must have been salvaged from the town dump where many of the prisoners laboured. The chandeliers were made of thousands of tiny strips of cardboard covered with silver paper and suspended by almost invisible threads. The Stations of the Cross had been crafted of tiny bits of coloured paper snipped from old magazines.

In the presence of death and unrelieved misery, these soldiers of the Red Army, officially classified as "atheistic Communists," had built a church from the gleanings of the town's trash cans. Like the barber shop at Grosshartmannsdorf, and the barnyard at Gross Selten, it was yet another wondrous anomaly.

For the first few days after their arrival, the Russians had paid us little attention beyond arranging for the food supplies from Fort Zinna. They were much too busy with their great offensive against Berlin, and there were still sporadic outbursts of fighting in the heavily wooded areas in the immediate vicinity of the camp. But eventually the propaganda corps from Moscow caught up with the front, and we were singled out for a little diplomatic attention.

Major Ledbedev, the Russian in charge of the camp, announced to the senior Allied officer one morning that the Russians were planning an evening of music and entertainment, together with a dance, and that fifty officers of the Allied forces were invited to attend.

The names of the several hundred British, American, Norwegian, Polish and French officers in the camp were put in a hat for a draw. I found myself among the winning fifty and was at once caught up in the sort of excitement felt by high school girls primping for the prom. Both British and American senior officers were concerned that we should make a good impression.

"Boys, it's got to be 'officers and gentlemen,' remember. Some of us arrived here in better dress than others — we'll have to dig around the camp and find as close to fifty decent uniforms as will fit you all. And for God's sake, don't let our side down. Those bastards will be watching your every move. Officers and gentlemen, remember?"

Come the exciting date, and we were dressed almost as if on parade back home. It was surprising how many Allied aircrew had landed in Germany in their parade-ground best. Among the Yanks there was the celebrated crew who had overshot their Fortress on a ferry flight across the Atlantic and had made a perfect and uneventful landing at an air base near Berlin. They were not alone. Not a few prisoners, who had made similar mistakes, had entered Stalag Luft 3 with their suitcases in their hands.

A Russian officer greeted us at the door of the barrack that had been cleaned out and refurbished to make a dance hall. As we entered we were paired off with one of those somewhat forbidding Russian front-line fighting females. None of them had the good fortune to be dressed in parade-ground tunics, as we were. They were big girls, most of them, and few of them seemed to be wearing any uniform cut or colour of skirt and blouse.

In two items of apparel, however, they were all identically dressed. Every one of them wore around her waist a big black leather belt. The belt buckle wore the insignia that had become all too familiar to all of us — a swastika and the bold lettering *"Gott mit uns."* Belts taken from fallen Germans were the prized souvenirs of front-line service. Every active Russian woman soldier was expected to have one.

And they all wore the same style of boot, equally familiar to us. But the German officers who had worn these smart black Wellingtons could never have worn them with the same proud swagger as the girls who had taken them from them. We looked at the belts and boots and admired what was in them. And we couldn't help trying to imagine just exactly how these girls had acquired them.

The Russians had conjured up an orchestra, made up of Italian prisoners, to provide the dance music. We had no way of knowing whether the Italians were being paid for their evening's perfor- mance, or whether they had been commandeered. In any event they played loudly, well and with a great Latin abandon.

Master of ceremonies for the evening was a Russian captain who sat not far from the musicians in a huge, overstuffed armchair. He, like the fighting females, wore a *"Gott mit uns"* belt. There was an open bottle of vodka on the floor beside his chair, from which he took frequent healthy swigs, and he was keeping time to the music by banging the tip of a German cavalry officer's sabre on the floor. He would have made an admirable Cossack brigand for the Hollywood stage.

My dancing partner made me nervous.

She was a half-inch taller than I, which may have been because of the boots she had stripped from the German she had liquidated, and she was wearing her pistol. The size of the holster and the uncovered butt end suggested it was a Magnum .45. I had never in my life danced with a girl wearing a loaded gun. On looking about the floor, I discovered that several of the other young women were also toting their guns.

As a dance, the evening was not a great success. There is nothing dainty about German army high boots, and my toes suffered several times. I couldn't talk to my partner; we could only look at each other and grin, and I am sure she felt as foolish and out of place as I did. I excused myself several times to visit the table that had set up as a bar. The supply of vodka was generous, and I had always been a more accomplished drinker than dancer.

The evening ended early.

Two of our fifty were Polish officers, and our Russian hosts had quickly identified them. They were surrounded by curious Russians who quite obviously were interested in how these Polish officers felt about the prospective political disposition of Poland, which had already fallen under the military rule of the Soviets.

Several times I caught a glimpse of our Polish friends. They were trying their best to appear comradely but were obviously not too happy about the situation. The Russians had had a long head start on the vodka and were pressing their fraternal attentions to the point of embarrassment.

It was when the shots rang out that we decided it was time to excuse ourselves and leave. There was really nothing threatening about the shots. It was simply that one of the Russians, with his arm around the shoulder of one of the Poles, was seeking to emphasize "the eternal friendship of Russians and Poles." As the Poles explained it to us later, each time the Russian slapped him on the back and declared that they were "Slav brothers," he had underscored the idea with a shot into the ceiling.

Back in our barrack bunks we could hear the party roaring until late at night, and we were quite satisfied to be "home."

XVII

Christel Achtelik

We were midway through the Battle of Berlin when I met Christel Achtelik. My mind is crowded with memories of that day. The first, one of the sharpest, is of two middle-aged women gathering spring flowers in a field flanking the main highway between Lucken-walde and Potsdam. It was only a few days after the Russian breakthrough across the Oder and about as long before the collapse of the Third Reich.

Memory falters on the kind of flowers the

women were picking. I think they were little yellow
things. But I recall quite clearly the colour of the
machine-gun tracers etching a lazy trajectory over
the women's shawled heads. It was orange-red.

The Russians had set up machine guns and
mortars in the ditch alongside the highway and
were firing at unseen targets in the pine woods on
the other side of the big field. Elements of General
Busse's Ninth Army were holding out in the woods,
hoping desperately to break out for a dash to the
Elbe and sanctuary in the West. There were still
about twelve thousand of them, and they were
making it difficult for the Russian armour and
transport moving up the highway to the Berlin
front.

We had an excellent view of it all from the
camp. We were officially "liberated" now, but
liberation was only a word. The battle flowed
around us, behind us and over us. We had no
choice but to watch and listen to the noise of
history.

It was while watching the women gathering the
spring flowers that I was struck by the strange surrealism of the scene. It was all bizarrely beautiful,
like a dream in slow motion. There was the sunshine and the blue sky, and the moist warmth of
the earth, and the fresh greenery of April. The mortars fired at spaced intervals, and there was a deep
silence between the shots. Once more, as on the
magical train ride through Hameln, I understood
the art of Salvador Dali.

The two women were quite unmoved by the
gunfire. A few seconds after each shot there was a
detonation in the woods and a splintering sound of

shattered trees. The machine guns chattered in the short measured bursts that marked the fire of seasoned gunners, and the tracers drifted lazily across the fields, arcing high over the women's heads and into the trees.

We ventured on foot beyond the camp boundary that day. It had been the order of the senior Allied officer that the prisoners, for their own safety, should remain within the wire, a sanctuary from the dangerous and shifting battleground. There were Russian guards around the perimeter, but they were human; they were not insensitive to the yearning of long-confined men for some small, limited taste of freedom. They looked the other way when we trickled through the wire to explore the exciting wonderland beyond.

Will Higgins shared my first breath of freedom that morning. We were both air force, with an itch to savour once more that unique and undefinable smell of aircraft, so we headed for the nearby Luftwaffe air strip. There was little left but wreckage. The hangars were a mass of collapsed roofing and twisted girders, and a lingering wisp of smoke trailed above the ashes of a barrack block. Dozens of shattered aircraft, including some gliders, littered the tarmac.

There was no one around but a group of schoolboys, applying their cheerful energy to dismantling some of the wrecked aircraft. One of them was busily removing the perspex canopy from over the cockpit of a glider.

"A cab for my wagon," he explained. "I'll have the best wagon in Luckenwalde."

We asked the boys why they weren't at school.

The schools had still been open during the time we had spent at the railway yards, when the children had sung *Baa! Baa! Black Sheep* for us. But now, with the guns hammering all around us, it was a stupid question. The boys stopped what they were doing and one of them giggled; then they all looked at each other and laughed.

"Russians shot the schoolmaster," one said.

We weren't shocked at their laughter. So the schoolmaster was dead. But it was a fine April morning, and school was out, and the boys were free to pillage a military airfield with all its fascinating wonders. They were young and healthy, and life was good. Somehow it was easy to forgive them for laughing. We had to laugh too.

We wandered away from the airfield and stopped to watch some hungry displaced labourers digging up a farmer's newly planted seed potatoes. Then we strolled through the woods and came upon a big fish-pond in what seemed to be a pleasant private estate. Some prisoners were there, trying to fish with threads and bent pins. They weren't having much luck until a Russian soldier happened along and lobbed a hand grenade into the pond. In moments the pond was silvered over with fish. There would be fresh fish with the beans back at the Stalag that night.

A little later that morning we met Christel Achtelik. The Achteliks lived not far from the Stalag, in the Weinberge, a little row of charming, middle-class homes nestled on a wooded slope overlooking Luckenwalde.

A girl of about eighteen, wearing a bright print

apron and fussing over some spring bulbs, was out in front of the house. We stopped, and in our best *kriegsgefangenen Deutsch*, remarked what a pleasant spring day it was. The girl responded, using her high-school English, and then her mother came to the door. We brought out our Red Cross cigarettes, Lucky Strikes. After we had talked a little more, and the mother seemed to have decided that we were civilized people, she invited us into the house.

When we sat down in the kitchen I suddenly found myself struggling to hold back tears. After all these years I was once more in a woman's kitchen, and it seemed more than I could bear. It was all there, just as it used to be when we were children. There was the kitchen stove and the kitchen smell, the pots and pans shining on the wall, pretty print curtains at the window, and the comfortably worn cushions on the kitchen chairs.

But I think it was mostly the aprons, the vision of two women in aprons, that brought me so close to tears. Life had magically become warm and wonderful and close. The mother put the kettle on the stove, and the daughter, Christel, brought out cups and saucers. They were real cups and saucers, decorated with pretty gold curlicues — not at all like the big, ugly earthenware Reich mugs we used in the camp.

We had mint tea, green and savoury, and smoked more Lucky Strikes. Christel introduced her small sister, Barbara, who was five, and told us about their father. Herr Achtelik was in the *Kriegsmarine*, serving in submarines. They had heard from him last from Kiel, but that had been six months ago.

Will and I told them where we came from, and about our families, and how we hoped we might be going home soon. We hardly talked at all about the war, because it was all around us, and there was nothing to say about it.

The Stalag had never seemed so wretched and dreary as it did that afternoon when we arrived back from Christel's place. The stench of stale sweat and musty bedding, potatoes and sour bread was something we had not noticed before.

Since we had been given access to the supplies at Fort Zinna there had developed a glut of bean soup in the camp. Will and I found a four-litre stone crock, filled it with soup and then carried it through the wire, across the fields and through the woods to Christel's place. We knew the Achteliks had little to eat. The battle was not yet over, and there had been no time to organize food supplies for the civilian population.

And so it was that the Achtelik kitchen became an enchanting refuge for us. Each day we waited patiently in the Stalag for the noon issue of the bean soup; then we set out for the Weinberge with the big stone crock. In the meantime the battle had been slowly ebbing away from Luckenwalde. Only during the night did we hear a desultory rattle of machine-gun fire as little groups of German infantrymen made a gambling dash across the highway in the faint hope of reaching the Elbe. Some made it, some helped to fill the town hospital, and others found a hiding place with the townsfolk.

It was not until our fourth or fifth daily

pilgrimage that I sensed a shadow over our visits.
Twice Christel had not been at home when we arrived with the soup, and for some reason her
mother had seemed just a little ill at ease.

She chatted pleasantly enough, served the
mint tea and welcomed us with as much maternal
warmth as if we had been her sons. Yet there was
no mistaking, barely beneath the surface, some
measure of anxiety and disquiet. On those occasions when Christel blew in I couldn't miss that
millisecond exchange of glances between the two
women, nor Christel's effort to mask some obvious
embarrassment.

As Higgins and I talked about it on our way
back to camp that afternoon, an explanation came
readily to mind.

"I know what's wrong, all right," I said. "These
are good, solid, respectable German townsfolk. You
know, the kind who wouldn't want to be 'talked
about' in their nice, middle-class community. After
all, regular visits from two strange men? They
want to be nice to us, but maybe it's not fair. They
may feel, well, compromised."

Higgins agreed with me. And so, reluctantly,
we determined not to visit the little house in the
Weinberge anymore.

For me, it was a grievous decision that was hard
to accept. Perhaps I am a weak character, for the
following day, after Higgins had been drafted for
loading duty at Fort Zinna, I was overwhelmed by
the thought of Christel's kitchen. When the soup
issue came at noon, I filled the stone crock once
again and set out for the Weinberge.

Christel's mother was there as usual, and little

Barbara was playing outside. Frau Achtelik poured the bean soup into several smaller containers, we had a cigarette, and she made a cup of mint tea.

Appearing even more agitated than before, she made a brave stab at small talk, and then, suddenly, with tears in her eyes, the truth came stumbling out.

"I have to tell you now," she cried, with a kind of anguish in her voice. "It's Christel . . . she is afraid you will be angry with her, about the soup . . . it's the soup."

I looked at her stupidly.

Please don't be angry with her," she continued. "We didn't have that soup. Christel has been taking it to the men . . . our soldiers . . . and the wounded. Please, don't be angry with her."

Once more I was close to tears in that kitchen. Captivity, as most of us discovered, brought feelings close to the surface; emotions were easily touched. Christel suddenly assumed a new and tenderly heroic dimension in my eyes.

I remembered that nocturnal machine-gun fire as General Busse's boys of the German Ninth Army tried to make it across the highway. Some of them had made it through the Russian fire, some were holed up in Luckenwalde wherever they could find shelter, and many of them were wounded. Christel had been playing big sister and Florence Nightingale for her embattled and wounded compatriots. I told Frau Achtelik there was nothing to be forgiven; we could both be proud of her daughter.

Many, many months later, back home in Canada when the war was only a memory, I received a letter from Christel. When I opened the envelope a photograph dropped out. It was a picture of Christel and her little sister, Barbara. My wife happened to be at my side. She picked up the photo, and with an arch glance and a feigned note of shock, said: "Is this your German family?"

She was only joking, of course, but somehow or other that is the way I remember them.

XVIII

Going Home

"Jeez! Will you look at these guys? They're eating that bread like it's cake."

We had just arrived in Halle, in American-held territory west of the Elbe, and within a half-hour were being fed by wide-eyed GIs as we hadn't been fed in years. The fluffy white crusty bread, fresh from the mobile bakery, did indeed taste like cake.

After a full month with the Russians at Luckenwalde, we had finally been trucked to the Elbe, had

walked the long, pontoon bridge to the U.S. side
and then had been whisked to the big Luftwaffe
training base that the Americans had taken over as
a POW reception centre.

The Yanks gave us a characteristic all-out
American welcome. Nothing was overlooked. Lined
up and waiting for us were the unbelievably effi-
cient mobile laundry, which gathered up our filthy
rags and returned them cleaned and ironed in a
matter of hours, the Red Cross van with everything
from toothbrushes to pajamas, and a mobile PX
with fabulous stores of chocolate bars, cigarettes
and a thousand other goodies, all for free.

But that reception at Halle is one I find
memorable for one particularly vivid scene, which
added to the drama of my German odyssey.

We had dismounted from the trucks in which
we had travelled from the Elbe, and a couple of
junior officers had marshalled us into military formation in a great courtyard flanked by towering
buildings of grey stone. The building we faced
presented an almost unbroken facade of stone, with
scarcely a window in the entire wall. It would have
done justice to a Hollywood set for a baronial castle.
At ground level the only break in the stonework
was a single small door, almost medieval with its
mellow planks and iron studs.

The stage was set.

The tiny door in the massive wall opened and
he stepped out to face us. He was a handsome and
debonair young major in the U.S. Army, about to
welcome us and give us an "orientation" talk on
the function and resources of the centre. He looked

as if he had just stepped off the parade ground at West Point; he was immaculately dressed, his shoes shined, buttons shined, and trousers creased to perfection, his service ribbons burning on the breast of a well-fitting tunic. He paced off about twenty smart steps in our direction and snapped to a halt facing us.

He looked as if he felt good about himself, and he had every right to be. As he flashed a smile at us and began to talk, we knew he was enjoying his role as host to newly liberated prisoners. He spoke well. The elocution was flawless, his explanations simple and unambiguous. He knew what he was doing, he was in command of the situation, and he was enjoying his position and his responsibility. We couldn't help but admire his stance.

He couldn't see the door opening behind him, the same door from which he had emerged. We could hear him talking, but suddenly all our hundreds of pairs of eyes were riveted on the woman who had just stepped out of that door.

We were like the proverbial birds watching a snake. We were fascinated.

It was like the climactic scene from a play, the denouement. The setting was perfect. The hero was centre stage, a figure of composure and pride but tragically oblivious to the fate that was overtaking him.

She wore the uniform of the U.S. Women's Army Corps; she was a WAC officer. But the buttons of her tunic were undone, she wore no tie, her shirt was open at the neck, and the neckline more than plunged. Her service cap was missing, and untidy strands of dark hair straggled down one side of her face.

She was drunk, and she swayed unsteadily as she closed in on her quarry. We were spellbound. Something quite terrible, some awful embarrass-ment, was about to happen, but we were powerless to intervene. Like some awful Greek tragedy, it had to be played out.

The major was warming to his subject, project-ing an aura of charm and command, when she reached him. He had no warning. She flung herself against him and grabbed him about the neck. Her husky, liquored voice echoed across the ancient courtyard.

"Aw, cut it out, Major. Come on back in and have a drink."

We felt suddenly demeaned and helpless. We suffered for him. We could see the self-assurance and pride draining from his face. There was no blush of embarrassment; only a crushed look of confusion and humiliation. He had been trans-formed in seconds to a spectacle of ridicule.

He made a feeble stab at recovery, still facing us while trying to shake the woman loose.

"That's about it, fellas . . . aw . . . aw . . . and, fellas, welcome home!"

Nobody said a word. We watched in stunned, pained silence as he led the woman away, and the two of them disappeared behind the old oaken door.

"Poor son of a bitch, my heart bleeds for him."

It was George Harsh, who was standing next to me. George was like that; his was a sensitivity born of years of personal suffering. He could feel for others as few men can.

And it was George who, on that first night in Halle, after the appalling embarrassment in the courtyard, had suggested that the two of us take a look around the town on the chance that we might find something to drink. Liquor was one item that the American army's hospitality failed to cover.

Most of the old city of Halle was in ruins. We found the vista of ripped-open tenement blocks, upended tramcars and cratered pavements depressing. Most of the population seemed to have deserted the place; the streets were virtually empty of humanity. There was little sign of activity of any kind, and a foreboding stillness hung over the place like a spell of doom.

It was not until we came to the banks of the River Saale that we saw a sign of life. On the other side of the river smoke rose thickly from the chimney of a long complex of factorylike buildings flanking the river. We came across a boy toying with a rowboat at the river's edge and asked him about the building across the river.

"*Ist eine Brauerei,*" he told us.

We couldn't wait. We handed the boy a pack of Camels, and he was happy to row us across to the brewery. There was a small door and a bell in the high brick wall that surrounded the place. After we had rung the bell and waited for a few moments, an elderly man came to the door. We told him we were two prisoners of war on our way home, holding out a packet of Camels as we spoke. Was there some way we might find a drink?

He laughed, took the cigarettes and invited us inside to his office. It appeared that he was the chief night watchman, and that he had been employed at this brewery for the past twenty-six years, ever since he had been demobilized from the German army in 1919. Proudly he showed us some framed photographs on the office wall. In several of them he appeared in the typical group shots of servicemen. He was wearing the spiked helmet of the old kaiser's army.

He brought us some beer, poured it into big, handsome steins and began reminiscing about that faraway war in which he had fought. We didn't want to say too much about the war just finished, but we couldn't help remarking how miraculous it was that with most of the city of Halle in ruins, the brewery was still in full production.

He laughed, not without a note of pride.

"*Ach*, wars come, wars go — breweries, they go on forever!"

One feature of the Luftwaffe base at Halle captured the attention of all of us. It was the little Lutheran chapel on the base. On one wall, close by the altar, was a bronze plaque. It recalled that among the cadets of the old original Luftwaffe who had trained here during World War I were the following:

Manfred von Richthofen
Max Immelman
Oswald Boelcke
Lothar von Richthofen
Bruno Loerzer
Hermann Göring

They had been the German greats in that first, more chivalrous, more romantic, less violent war in the air, in an age untouched by the vile nihilistic politics that came to sully the feats of a later, armed Germany. Both wars had come and gone; soon nothing would be left but bronze plaques to commemorate it all.

There was one last stop on the way home to Britain. From Halle we were flown in U.S. Dakotas to Brussels, where there was to be a one-night stopover before we should be gathered up by the Royal Air Force and flown home to England.

For most of us, Brussels remains a somewhat hazy memory. Upon arrival at the airfield, we were paraded in businesslike fashion before a paymaster, who issued to each one of us a reasonably generous advance on our London pay accounts. From there we had to run a somewhat embarrassing gauntlet of Medical Corps nurses who sprayed antivermin powders into crotches and armpits. Funded and disinfected, we were let loose on Brussels.

The highlight of the evening was a reception in the ballroom of the erstwhile royal palace where we were to spend the night. Behind the long bar, attended by barmaids recruited from the Brussels equivalent of the Junior League, cases of whisky marked "Property of the First Canadian Army" were stacked to the ceiling. Other varieties of alcohol were in equal supply, and all of it was free.

It was at Brussels that we last saw Dr. Monteuis. I chatted with him briefly at the reception, where I found him relaxing in a corner surrounded by bottles of champagne. I didn't see him again until the following morning, when we woke in our cots in the corridor of the old palace. The headaches were epidemic; many of the boys were in extremis.

But good old Doc Monteuis was with us to the last, cheerful and conscientious. Moving solicitously from cot to cot, his pockets bulging with bottles of the best brandy, he was still ministering to our needs.

"This is the last medicine you'll ever have from me, boys. Open your mouth and say ah-a-a-ah!"

That day vied with the day of liberation in high emotion. I made the flight home to England in the bomb aimer's bay of a Lancaster bomber. I never got to meet and know the pilot of that aircraft, but he must have been a man of imagination and great feeling. As we approached the edge of the European mainland the Lancaster steadily lost height until we found ourselves flying at a height of only a few hundred feet along the beach at Dunkirk.

It was like being at a movie and seeing the part where you say to yourself, "This is where I came in." For this was Dunkirk. The beaches were still strewn with burned-out vehicles and litter of every kind, and dozens of shattered hulls lay awash in the shallows beyond. Here, too, the Spirit of Man had vanquished.

There was one more thrill that pilot gave us. From Dunkirk, still flying at low level, he headed the Lancaster westward across the sea. A short time later there was a gentle roll and a dip of wings, and we saw the White Cliffs of Dover dead ahead.

To me, they seemed a little blurred, but actually they hadn't changed a bit.

Epilogue

It was many years later. I was back home in Nova Scotia, a guest at one of those business-oriented cocktail parties, the kind where you are expected to mingle, talking to one person after another all the time balancing a glass in your hand and trying to keep it filled without anyone noticing how many times you have circled the bar.

As can happen on such occasions, it was the presence of a young woman that made the evening memorable. She was wearing a gentle, enchanting

263

smile as she approached me through the throng.

"Aren't you . . . ?"

I told her, yes, I was, and tried desperately to remember where I had met her before. Or even whether I had ever met her before. It would be so embarrassing not to remember anyone so charming. But she quickly put me at ease.

"You don't know me," she said. "But I've known you for a long, long time. But you wouldn't know anything about that."

It all sounded a little puzzling.

"As a matter of fact," she said, "I used to pray for you every day."

It had been a long time ago, she said, during World War II. She had been a little girl attending one of those red one-room schoolhouses in rural Cape Breton.

"I think you know my Uncle Jasper," she said.

That rang a bell. Jasper Ferguson was a Cape Bretoner who had served in the air force and with whom I had spent my three years in Stalag Luft 3. Yes, I certainly remembered her Uncle Jasper.

"Well, I was just a small girl when Uncle Jasper went off to war, and we were all so proud of him. He joined the air force and went overseas, and then we used to have letters from him when he was with Bomber command.

"Then one day he was reported missing. We all felt so terrible about it. A little later we heard that Uncle Jasper was a prisoner of war. We were happy to know he was alive, but we worried all the same. We just didn't know what might happen to him in a German prison camp.

"Well, the day after we heard about him being in the prison camp, I was on my way to school. It was a long walk along a country road, and we had to cross a little bridge over a brook.

"That morning I stopped on the bridge. I picked up a pebble from the road, dropped it into the brook and said a little prayer for Uncle Jasper. And after that I did the same thing every morning."

More letters had come from Uncle Jasper in Germany, and soon they learned that other airmen from Nova Scotia had arrived in Stalag Luft 3.

"So then I dropped more pebbles into the brook each morning and said a prayer for each of them.

"There was Vince Mancini and Mike Whalley and Pinkie Gaum, all from Sydney, and Al Langille from Baddeck, and Law Power. We didn't know any of them, but I had their names from Uncle Jasper's letters. So every morning I would drop the pebbles in the brook and say my prayers for them. By the time the war ended, I was dropping seven pebbles into the brook every morning."

She stopped and gave me that gentle smile again.

"I just thought you'd like to know that you were one of my pebbles."

About the Author

Kingsley Brown is a native of Toronto. He was educated in England and Canada, and began his newspaper career as a reporter with *The Toronto Star* in 1928. Newspapering took him to Winnipeg, Halifax, Hamilton and Saint John, where for three years he was managing editor of the *Telegraph-Journal*. His flying career dates from his pre-war membership in the Halifax Aero Club, and his air force service began the day World War II was declared, September 3, 1939. During the Diefenbaker years, he served as Special Assistant to Canada's first woman cabinet minister, the Honourable Ellen Fairclough. Until his retirement in 1978, he was Director of Development at St. Francis Xavier University. He now lives at his seaside home near Antigonish, Nova Scotia.